"Dr. Cox is an amazing wordsmith, and this book is a precious gem. He combines wisdom and humor to teach us about our last lap of our earthly race. It is a reminder of the impermanence of this physical life, the importance to invest in our spiritual, eternal life and 'lay up our treasures in heaven.'"

—DONNA AMES, Professor Emeritus, Department of Psychiatry and Biobehavioral Sciences, UCLA

"This book is filled with a mouthful of humor, a headful of wisdom, and a heartful of compassion. It will at the same time excite your mind, make you think, and understand a bit more about your loved ones and your future."

—JAMES M. MASON, Experimental Pathologist

"This book is hilarious but will chill your soul with the truth."

—ANN CRAWFORD, Nanogenarian

"*Geezers and Goozers* is a delightful and heartwarming collection of life lessons that offers valuable insights for everyone. Its charm and originality make it truly exceptional and inspiring."

—ERIN KOEHNE., Lt. Col., US Army

"*Geezers and Goozers* is a delightful book about the foibles of increasing years. It humorously and sensitively addresses many issues we face with sound psychological information and common sense. It will bring tears to your eyes from laughing and the sensitive spots it touches. A brilliant treatise on this stage of life."

—SHIRLEY BURNSIDE, Family Therapist

"Funny but not funny at all, when you are getting old like I am. This is a book to take to heart and read over again."

—RANCE GERRINGER, Paint and Interior Design Consultant

"Subtle and nostalgic hew-haws from yesterday, soul filling and memory tingling. Great to share with your kin folk!"

—LEE ATKINSON, Physicist, Meanstride Technologies

"Thank you for letting me read *Geezers and Goozers*. So much of the reality is seen here. Please know that your words are appreciated and need to be shared."

—BETSY BALDWIN, Artist Educator, Retired

"Aside from being humorous and enjoyable, *Geezers* is a must read for anyone who will experience aging within the family, via friends, or one's own self. Drawing from decades of professional personal experiences, Dr. Cox, now a geezer himself, delivers a humanistic and teaching guidebook on our aging populations."

—BETH LOEBER ELSWICK, Professional Musician, and James Elswick, Professional Musician

"Thanks for sharing this book. It is entertaining reading with many words of wisdom."

—ED MCCAULEY, Retired President, North Carolina Hospital Association

GEEZERS and GOOZERS

GEEZERS and GOOZERS

All I Need to Know I Learned from Old People

RICHARD H. COX

Forewords by
Rebecca Ann Schmidt *&* David R. Cox

Denouement by
Joanna Sue Causley

RESOURCE *Publications* • Eugene, Oregon

Resource Publications
An Imprint of Wipf and Stock Publishers
199 W. 8th Ave., Suite 3
Eugene, OR 97401

www.wipfandstock.com

PAPERBACK ISBN: 979-8-3852-4854-4
HARDCOVER ISBN: 979-8-3852-4855-1
EBOOK ISBN: 979-8-3852-4856-8

VERSION NUMBER 112125

This book is affectionately dedicated to the thousands of dear older people that have blessed and enhanced my life.

"All to the jaundiced eye is yellow"

—ALEXANDER POPE

CONTENTS

FOREWORD
—*Rebecca Ann Schmidt*

UNDERNEATH HIS DEGREES, ACCOLADES, and other achievements, this author has collected over 96 years of life, and is a real-life geezer, who just happens to be my father. Through his example, I have learned how to find the silver lining in the darkest of clouds and the satire and humor in the most horrible of situations. May you, the reader, also find the silver lining and humor as you chuckle, shed a tear, and even belly-laugh while reading his life recollection of true stories.

FOREWORD
—David R. Cox

"WRITING CAN BE THERAPEUTIC," they say. As a psychologist and author in his "pre-geezer stage," I have also taken up songwriting. I find it therapeutic. I find the songs of my fellow songwriters to be heartening, funny, sad, and you name it. As I listen, I identify with several and they touch me in a way that is difficult to express- as in striking a chord in my soul. Richard has written music, but to my knowledge it has always been instrumental. Herein are some of the lyrics missing from his many previously published musical works, some of the stories behind the songs. Just as with songs, you won't find all of them to your liking. But some may strike a chord with your soul. Enjoy.

PREFACE

I'M TOLD THAT TO be proper a book needs a preface. I wouldn't know why, since that too, from my years of looking at tomes of words, in mold-odor filled libraries, is likely to be seen as irrelevant book filler. Few people spend much time reading the preface of any book. But, in a half-hearted attempt to be academically acceptable, if that is possible when writing for a totally unknown audience, here is the preface:

I'm just a geezer talking about geezers (old men) and goozers (old women), but for nearly 50 of my 96 years on this earth, my wife, with whom I shared a beautiful life of 70 years of marriage, (a brighter than I, PhD psychologist), and I, a guy educated way beyond his intelligence,(MD, PhD, etc.) served as administrators, practitioners, and professors. We were also consultants to retirement villages and nursing homes all over the United States. If that were not immersion enough into the crony world, we lived in two of them. I live in one now and find it exemplary and a wonderful place to enjoy my "over-time" years. We worked in facilities that were "for-profit," "not-for-profit," church-related, non-church related, government run, privately operated, and all mixtures in-between. There were commonalities among them all, mostly the stories.

The stories in this book are placed at random, intentionally. The sad ones, if told all at one time would simply be too much to bear. Life can be hard at the end, and it is so very important to keep it lightened up, with humor and as much joy, as much as possible.

Laughter is still the best medicine. Physical pleasures that we have counted on for all of life gradually slip away, and little joys take on much more meaning. Things previously taken for granted begin to be extremely important and appreciated. The smile, the compliment, the greeting, or the simple, "hello" of a friend is the soul's emollient to many lonesome elders.

We met many geezers and goozers, and we were two of them, just like them in most ways. Being critical and humorous at the same time was not difficult. Every day was new with new, intriguing events, but in most ways only variations of the previous day. Many met new friends every day, since they didn't remember meeting them yesterday and the day before that as well.. Others told new stories, that were only new to them, because they didn't remember having told the same story every day for months. But some were very clever and could make additions and subtractions to previous events and make everyone laugh. Others were depressed and said, "Life is over, why am I still here?"

Many persons, particularly geezers, love to tell jokes. The art of joke-telling is not a gift possessed by all. Lots of old folks don't realize they lack that gift and bore you anyway and are amazed when you don't laugh. But even those who have enjoyed this gift, are frustrated in old age, since they often remember the joke but forget the punch line. However, Joe, is different. He remembers the punch line and has to ask if anyone remembers the joke! His repertoire of jokes is by now all very well cataloged by all the geezers in their own joke libraries.

At one time, we seriously considered selling our home and traveling around the US in an RV writing a book as result of our consulting in "homes for the aged." But, with both of us being piano players, we just couldn't face the thought of giving up our grand piano, and what do you do with a beloved library of books that are just part of you? That was probably an okay choice though, since now I can write all those memories in much more comfort. In real time they would not have been nearly as interesting, and entirely too accurate. Human interest stories are a bit like many culinary creations, the longer they sit, the longer the spice keeps working.

Now, my legitimate writing colleagues tell me that I need to make some disclaimers, if I'm going to be as forthright as I cannot help but be. So, here goes:

Disclaimer One

The stories in this book are all true stories, although memory may have altered the details of their actual happenings. You see, if you write as a nonagenarian (a person in their 90's), it is not only age that becomes "non," but also time, place, memory, and communication skills. It's really difficult to be true when writing. Like I said, all the stories are actual happenings, just sometimes mixed-up versions of each other, with lots of disguise to protect my safety! Truth is indeed stranger than fiction, but then, fiction is only a mishmash of truth. And truth is still stranger than fiction, and certainly usually much funnier, when not tragic.

Trying to remember which character belonged to which play, is not only impossible, but doing so would greatly impinge upon the entertainment value of this writing. In spite of this, every story is in fact much truer, than not. It's just that I'd like to keep the few friends I have in my rapidly decreasing population, even though most of them, like myself, are just a bunch of hanging-on dotards. I try to stay away from repetition, but most of life is a series of repetitions with minor variations. It seems that the music of life's years is composed of only a few songs, but lots of verses.

Disclaimer Two

The people in this book are real, and, have real names. Or, at least at one time were real. You see, when you are a nonagenarian, there aren't too many folks still around your age, so your focus is a bit fuzzy about the "real" ones that are, I mean that were, in your life. Some of them are still there. All are still here through their stories. That is how we ultimately survive, in the memories of those around us. I have thousands of friends, most of whom survive only in my memory. But since this writing spans many years and the stories have come from all over the United States, I really don't know how many, or in truth, if any at all, still survive in the body, save for a few in my current living arrangement. The older you get the fewer friends of your age you have. It's important to keep making younger friends, so you have some! Most of the new ones will be younger and either look up to you with compassion or pity.

Disclaimer Three

I have no delusions about this book ever being important to anyone. Well, some may find it an excuse to laugh a little, cry a little, feel happy, or sad, or, just need another book on the shelf to make it look like they read books. That doesn't matter. Writing is always more cathartic and therapeutic for the writer than those who will potentially read it. So, yes, I need both catharsis and the therapy.

Disclaimer Four

This item would normally be placed in "acknowledgements," but since anonymity and confidentiality is of ultimate importance, I can only thank the many who know, and the more who do not know, that they are in this book. If any were to recognize themselves, they would need to be literary schizophrenics to see the multiple parts, geography, and facts that are woven together. I can guarantee that some will try! Yes, I'm in there too, but of course refuse to identify which one is the person I remember as me!

Are four disclaimers enough? I think so; at any rate, that's all there are.

ACKNOWLEDGMENTS

I'D LOVE TO LIST the wonderful folks who are the stories in this book. But confidentiality, anonymity, and for heaven's sake, the caution against libel and lawsuit, prohibit such. So, folks, "thanks for the memory," as Bob Hope would say.

> *"Getting old doesn't matter, if you don't mind;*
> *If you lose your mind, then it doesn't matter!"*

AUTHORS' NOTE
The People Stories

AFTER OVER 96 YEARS of stubbing one's toe in this world, it's hard to sort out the things you've bumped into. Particularly the things you saw and experienced in those places where they send old people (some go there by their own choice; it keeps the kids from making unfortunate decisions). So, with no real organization, I'll launch into what I started to do before I was told to write an introduction and preface!

I can't always be sure where these stories occurred. But location is rarely important. It's always too rainy, not rainy enough, too much snow or none, or too hot or too cold. Having everything okay would just be too boring. The agenda for discussion among the inhabitants is pretty much the same. There are, however, some reliable issues such as the weather, bodily functions, the food (which is always too hot or too cold, too greasy or too dry), and I forgot, the helpings are too much, therefore wasteful, or too small, which means the administration is stingy or wasting money. Rumor and gossip ae not considered as such but, just entertaining truth, which reveals one's ability to improvise and make dull things exciting.

Although these stories are not cataloged by the month, it is easy to recollect them that way. The cold winters of the north and the hot months in the south sometimes entered into all kinds of stories. Oh, I forgot to tell you that my wife and I traveled the

United States consulting in "homes for the aged" which I'll talk about later. Almost no older person we met was happy with the weather, but it was the one constant in nearly every conversation. Weather is always "safe small talk." Religion and politics are bound to create disharmony, and you can only hold another's attention for so long talking about your grandkids, that no one except you really cares about. So, everything is a "bless your heart" moment when you must take everything with a grain of salt and make up your mind what it means.

Growing old with old people is a challenge. Everyone is in decline, and all are in need of various kinds of care. The places where these dilapidated bodies live are called all sorts of names, such as "Retirement Community," "Rest Home," etc., they are all pretty much the same, carefully disguised nurseries and funeral parlors. Since many wear diapers and must be fed, they fit the infancy model, and many of the others are in what is called "heaven's waiting room."

They all try to make life at least endurable as the grim reaper approaches, but they don't really fool anyone. These "homes" are, however, powerful magnets against one's life savings. Since many are "for profit" enterprises, there is sometimes little mercy for those who can't afford it. They end up in places that don't smell good, and the care is sketchy at best. The cost of aging is not cheap, and the dying process thrusts the final spear into one's bank account.

INTRODUCTION

THIS BOOK REALLY DOES not need an introduction. The up-front information, which is rarely read anyway, is embedded in the stories. Since you are reading this book, I can safely assume that like me, you are sufficiently prejudiced that there is no intended, or non-intended, attempt to dissuade anyone from any idea about old people. Since we all start to get old the moment we are born, I'm just talking to fellow travelers at different intersections along Life Route, US 101.

I do need to let you know right up front that my reason for telling these stories is more than just to entertain. Real life is made up of stories, funny stories, sad stories, true stories, and fabricated ones. These are not fabrications, but real stories slightly altered and mixed up to disguise identity.

Further, any puns that seem offensive are not to be taken that way. However, if the stories of our lives are robbed of their emotional blunders and foibles, whether funny or sad, they cease to represent reality. Deception is neither funny nor helpful, so none of these are intended to deceive. They are intended to make the reader laugh a little, commiserate a lot, and see if their "Sherlock Holmes" abilities are working to discover identity. Even though the reader may not know the actual owners of these stories, all seniors will know others that are like them.

My life has been continually enriched by old people. It was only through "old people" that I found my way. I have always been more comfortable around seniors than my own age group. When I taught Sunday School, I always chose to teach the Senior Class. Our family's best friends were older folks. All of the major influences in my life were older. When my wife was born, her mother was 45 years old, and her mother became one of my best friends and devoted supporters. She and my engaged girlfriend gave me my first fine trumpet. Nearly all the members of the first church I served as pastor were senior citizens, to whom I will always be grateful, for teaching me so much about life. It is no misstatement, when I say, "All I Need to Know, I Learned from Old People."

Since I'm prone to make up words, (I guess that makes me a neologist), I need to tell you that there is no word "goozers." But that's wrong, because now there is. I just made it up. After all, if we have "geezers" which traditionally refers to old men, then we must have a similar word for older women; so why not invent the word "goozers"! Actually, just to brag a bit about my neolgistic talents, a word I made up is in the Dictionary of Psychology, (Brunner/ Mazel, 1999, p. 626, "narapoia," the opposite of paranoid). Making up words makes people think, and since most person's vocabularies are limited, they don't recognize that it's just a "made up" word. They just think you are smarter than they are!

JANUARY

"I thought about quitting my old habits, but I don't want to be known as a quitter."
—THELMA, M.

Auld Lang Syne

THE NEW YEAR'S EVE party is the highlight. It takes a bit of creativity to keep elders engaged until midnight. So, they don't. They don't even try. The clocks are set at 9:00 p.m. when the party starts at 6:00 p.m., hence, midnight comes at 9:00 p.m.! It works. Punch and cookies, even some chocolate things, canned music with a couple live entertainers, a few old-groaner jokes by a few residents, and for those still in attendance at such a late hour, Auld Lang Syne on the piano at their fabricated "midnight" (9:00 p.m.).

There are still many "oldsters" that remember Guy Lombardo and his Royal Canadians big band that was known for striking the downbeat at midnight. The make believe is okay. For most, it is a blessing to at least see the dawn of another year. Geraldine at 93 still plays the piano, Merle attempts to sing, Leland shuffles as he steps on Helen's toes trying to dance, and those who aren't completely aware of where they are, shout "Happy New Year" at each other over the canned music, and decibels beyond their hearing aids!

New Year's Eve parties are a respite from the incessant boredom of everyday being the same. Some say that every day is

1

Saturday because they don't have to go to work. It lets both Geezers and Goozers forget their problems temporally and pretend they are young again. Most have a bit too much sugar in the "goodies," and sometimes way too much in "spirits." The loud music is way too much for their hearing aids, but they tolerate the cacophony and just talk louder. The Goozers often shed their shoes when the dancing starts, since their half-century old pointed, spike-heel pumps pinch the bunions on their feet. The Goozers mostly feel pressured into wanting to dance and give in, and some try to look like they are having fun, but the pain on their face gives them away.

The really great holidays are those that are fortunate to live in a more up-scale facility and the day is celebrated with a festive brunch, which includes New Year's Day. Incredibly well done, as they are in most places. Even the more budget facilities try to make the ay uplifting. A smorgasbord of healthy and not-so-healthy sugars, fats, and proteins are laid out in artistic fashion. Cuts of fine meat, and deserts of culinary excellence. And, to make it over-the-top, an in-house sommelier offers a glass of either red or white wine!

Those whose physical condition prohibits mobility to the dining room, room service is provided. Plates overflow with enough leftovers for soups and casseroles for days to come. In spite of sanitary concerns, much food will go back to apartments in bags, purses, or other semi-camouflaged containers.

There are a few problems that inevitably result from such festive occasions. There is Henry whose gout always flares up from food from too much uric acid, (he does love beef and red wine). Then there's Julie who claims that the sugars in her three-scoop ice cream pie-ala- mode bring on an arthritic attack. Ben always gets a bit tipsy if he can entice the wine-master into "just one more." Mac (for Maclellan), gets upset that while coffee keeps him awake, it also gives him "heartburn," but he drinks it anyway. And of course, Neal insists on drinking buttermilk with his black-eyed peas. Some claim that eating black-eyed peas ensures a prosperous New Year. Muriel is concerned that she dripped the chocolate sauce on her vintage white scarf, that carefully partially covers her multiple folds of an aged, wrinkled neck. Too bad that she and others do not see beauty in aging, and instead constantly attempt to disguise it.

Leland is a bit more pedestrian, because he says that almost everything, he eats gives him diarrhea. He'd like to trade with Haley (at least for a couple of days) since Haley gets constipated from almost everything. They openly trade their physiological journeys rather loudly while eating. That's how we know about them. It seems that they think others can't hear any better than they can.

Jeanne gets headaches from the artificially over-sweetened iced tea. She also argues, that it is an absolute abomination to have un-sweetened iced tea. No correctly bred Southerner would think of such. She is a retired RN and thinks that too much sugar is sinful, because it "puts on weight", and it's obvious she doesn't need any more evidence for that.

Everybody knows what "sweet tea should taste like." If you really want to make it authentic, she says you need to add just a little more sugar anyway! Two teaspoons full would be about right she says, but since sugar comes in those little paper packages, three of them should do. Bill is never happy with the lack of enough salt, so he adds it to everything including sausage! Jim, the many long years ago retired pharmacist insists that they are ensuring an early death by adding both salt and sugar. He sticks with "bloody Mary's"! The staff monitor him closely lest he become a inebriated Goozer.

Regional tastes rear their ugly head constantly. Like Jeanne insists, it's a mystery why a Northerner can't get used to "sweet tea." Randy, from North Carolina, like others previously mentioned, can often be seen adding sweetener to his already sweet tea, and to take the top off the saltshaker, because cooks in the South are just too accommodating to those with little good taste. To assure his care for healthy eating, he does not use sugar for the additions, but four packs of Splenda.

It is virtually impossible for a Westerner, or Northerner to eat vinegar-based bar-b-que. By the same token, only true Southerners understand why anyone would eat collards. But then, only those from Canada complain that there is no poutine. Very few

Southerners have ever heard of poutine. Those who have swear they wish they had not! Some find malt vinegar to be the savior of collards and other barely edible greens. Meat, of any variety, should be cooked till dead. They insist that everyone knows that meat with red still on it can give you worms. But then there's Libby that puts ketchup on her salad!

Moving from one geographic locale, particularly if you've lived there most of your life, can be stressful in the culinary department. But that is not the only department that suffers. Just at the time in life when you need, and start, to give away your over-stuffed closets of no-longer in-style, and no longer worn, clothes, you find that your "Southern" clothes won't work in Chicago, or your Chicago clothes don't do well in Georgia.

But since frugality is the religion of the day, even though many need not be so concerned, these vintage bits of haberdashery are worn anyway! So you see the "cultured" lady from Brooklyn wearing her mink stole when it is 50 degrees in the sun, and Lyle sporting his nylon leisure suit from the 50's.of course, sometimes they are vindicated sporting their winter attire since cold snaps do occur even in the South.

George and cold water

George, a widower Geezer, had been living alone for over five years in his apartment, but somehow noticed after all that time that he, and his facilities had changed. Now, there are several issues here that he had to face, adroitly. For one thing, most inhabitants are Goozers and would not understand, or if they did, they would care less, except what juicy conversations could emerge over tea. And, when addressing private issues, words are sometimes more hindrance than help.

Somehow, he had to explain that either his "parts" had morphed without his knowledge, or the bathroom facilities had been replaced. He tried to explain, to male administration, I might add, that he was having a problem with the "certain anatomical parts." Somehow the water level in the porcelain bowl was insufficiently individually adjustable. At times, when others just didn't seem to understand, he referred to such in strictly gross language as his "family jewels." Being an educated gentleman, he faced severe frustration with his inability to communicate his very personal consternation.

The kindly, but overly efficient male assistant administrator, reminded him that his jewelry was his responsibility. He sometimes could not make the reverse cognitive jump from his use of that phraseology, and what others might interpret it as being. Some of his cohorts had never heard of any being stolen, and furthermore, it was clearly spelled out in the Admission Package, that the "home" assumed no responsibility for such items. He should have given his jewelry away or put it in a safe. No one could figure out why his jewels were coming into contact with cold water!

He just couldn't explain it in "decent" language, but he kept trying. He tried to tell them that it was a problem with the latrine. The administrator, so much younger, had never heard of a latrine. But upon googling his cell phone discovered it is an "out-house." That complicated communication even further, since he kept his lawnmower, and garden tools in his out-house, which he called a shed. So, George tried another word, the "commode." Upon googling that word, which the young administrator didn't know either, he discovered it to be a piece of furniture containing a concealed chamber pot. This sounded more like kitchenware, so he suggested George speak to the kitchen staff, maybe they could help. The story did not end well. George passed from this mortal globe with unresolved issues around private matters that eluded his ability to explain.

Ubiquitous "Mabels"

Every "old folk's home" has a Mabel. Names carry meaning. Everyone knows that "Mables" are all like. They are gossips, nosey, and fastidious in an antique way. Some still use bluing to make their hair appear "whiter," baptize themselves daily in stale perfume, and somehow are everywhere at the same time. Their mobility is amazing, considering that most shuffle along behind a rollator. Modern sneakers adorn their ancient lace dresses. They can be found in any hallway, any tea parlor, at all meetings of any sort, and of course huddling in the dining rooms. I think academics call that ubiquitous. I've tried to lose them, but when you succeed in losing one, you immediately bump into at least two more. Some facilities have roaming security guards, but they are really quite unessential, since these roaming rumor accumulators are aware of every move of everyone at all hours of the day and night!

Some Geezers and Goozers have rollators and others attempt to set new records for mileage and speed with their battery-operated, non-road legal vehicles. These folks are sort of like Easter eggs, that is, you find them in the strangest places. They always find you first. Although not always, they tend to be females, i.e., Goozers. They have the unique ability to look surprised, knowing full well that you are expecting one of them in every shadow. I've learned, however, to give them credit, because they are unfathomable resources of information not available elsewhere. Single Goozers try to avoid them, since they are deathly afraid of being seen as an "available bachelor."

Audrey, the Sentry

Audrey, a Goozer widow, is an example of the self-appointed reporting Goozer par excellence, (most women in those places are widows), had an unusual gift. This particular "Mable," Sarah by real name, had moved from California to Colorado only a few years earlier, but she had amassed an enviable history of the place and its inhabitants in a short time. She could smell rumor and gossip a mile away. Her 84 years of Beagle sniffing skills were honed to perfection. She could be found at any hour of the day or night burning battery power, making the rounds on every floor, in every part of the multi-unit complex. She made a printed directory of residents totally unnecessary since you could always find her. A monthly newsletter was always out of date; she got there first.

Although Audrey was not the only member lf her surveillance staff, she set the bar very high for those who would compete with her. Like I said before, why the administration spent money on surveillance was a mystery when she was doing it for free. But then, it became clear that although her all-seeing eyes might be present, her reporting skills offered sufficient reason to doubt the accuracy of her reporting abilities, either because of dementia, or more likely, conscious choice.

Word had it that she had suffered at the hands of a non-loving husband for many years. No one in current residence had met him, so her word was truth. Her stories had probably been altered by need and time since his death, but who knew? She speaks of him as, "He left me seven years ago. . . ." The choice of words is telling. Indeed, he "left" her and may have threatened to do so on a regular basis. Although totally unfair, I'm sure it would be interesting to hear his side of the story. It might lead to commiserating with him.

A few years with her could encourage a butterfly to turn back into a worm, proving reverse metamorphosis! Some of the men who knew him insisted that when he was first married, he was nearly even feet tall but after several years of her battering, he stood at heaven's gate as all of five feet four!

All sound becomes something of a noise, when the inevitable presbycusis of aging takes its toll. Hearing aids are expensive excuses not to hear, and misunderstanding is often much more interesting than hearing what is really said. In all fairness, however, there is no such thing as a "good hearing aid." Such a term is a perfect oxymoron.

Just singing in the rain

My friend Ben loves sitting on his patio and people watching. It must be admitted that watching people, particularly the elderly, can be entertaining. In Colorado one could alternate being awed by the surrounding 14,000-foot-high peaks and the walkers, shufflers, and wheelers that went by. Jeanne had so much fun. It was no doubt less than fun for her, and probably, more than she'd realized, that a few Geezers were making her their most enjoyable incident of the day. It was raining. The wind was blowing in the opposite direction of where we were sitting, but, coming down in buckets on her.

She had been to the grocery store. Now, you have to get this picture in your head. She was holding an undersized umbrella over her roller-basket-cart, full of paper bags of groceries. One could see the Cornflakes, and the Graham crackers, toilet tissue, and 6 pack of Coke, but not much else. The reason it could be seen was because the bags were wet and coming apart. The sky was clearing, and if she would only wait a few minutes in her car, she could have avoided soggy Cornflakes and water-soaked Grahams.

No, the Geezers thought about helping her, but by the time they'd got to her across the parking lot, she would be inside. So, as always, others' misfortunes are sometimes one's grist for joy.

Past lives

There are so many real, and not-so-real, stories about the former lives of the residents. No one ever really knows, or probably really cares, but then, you can't just tell people you don't care about their past lives (even though you surely don't). Some are convoluted by memory, others by intent, and other are truly marvelous, while others are tragic. Those with living spouses sometimes had validation, but memory is not accurate either. It seems that the old statement, "upon all the rain must fall," is just not true.

Some Geezers and Goozers seem to get to their earthly end with only "good stuff," while other seem to have lived in a constant hurricane. Stories also grow with time. Stories also grow with time. Memories that might have been only brief rain-showers, become tornadoes when told many years later. Every story takes on a life of its own, and those who have heard the same story many times always enjoy hearing the new version.

Every generation produces unique variations in the vicissitudes of life. No one feels good about those who must live in the memory of the concentration camps, the terrors of war, the loss of the homestead by fire, the head-on crash that killed their only child, etc. But life's inevitable happenings seem to make some bitter, and others appreciative, of what did not happen that could have. Most, in honesty, in the present generation older folks are very grateful. They have lived through tough times and have come out as better people. Many well-corroborated stories are undeniably tragic, while others prove the repetition of humanness.

FEBRUARY

"My best medicine is WD-40"
—*EVERETT L.*

THE TIME BETWEEN NEW Year's Day and February goes fast. Old people claim that the older you get, the faster time goes. Soon after the New Year's Eve party and the New Year's Day "overeating" festivities, comes Valentine's Day. Believe it or not, pink candy hearts, Concern for those with diabetes does not exist. Valentine cards, red boxes of chocolates, pink candy hearts, and paper cutout hearts appear – by at least February 1st, just to make sure their decorative value is appreciated long enough. It is, however, sad for some who no longer have their "sweetheart," as it is joyful for those who are more fortunate.

Hearing "aids?"

All sound, becomes something of a difficult item when the inevitable presbycusis of aging takes its toll. Hearing aids are expensive excuses not to hear, and misunderstanding is often much more interesting than hearing what is really said. In all fairness, however, there is no such thing as a "good hearing aid." Such a term is a perfect oxymoron.

A full- lifetime of enduring hearing gadgets has given me more knowledge about them than I can share. I was born with no hearing in the right ear, and I'm told that I lost all but a small bit of hearing in my left ear due to simultaneous measles and mumps when six years old. So, a lifetime of hearing challenges is quite familiar territory. Yes, hearing aids are a blessing; most of the time. And life has doubtless been easier with them. They were not available when I was a youngster, so early life had its challenges. For instance, trying to hear the teacher who was facing the blackboard, and I had to rely on lip-reading. Or, getting teachers, parents, and friends to believe that you really did not hear them, and that you were not ignoring or disobeying them!

The greatest thing about hearing aids (other than hearing most of what you want to hear), is that you can turn them off, thus cutting out the gabber without insulting him or her. The inevitable siren-sounding feedback is nerve racking. The accumulated ear wax resulting from the "plug" in your ear is ugly, and just when you get the volume set to a comfortable level, someone yells at you, or a firetruck decides go by with the siren at full blast. It's sort of like getting your coffee "just so" with the right amount of cream and sugar, then the server comes by and ruins it by filling up your cup!

So, we must add the problems of music. Music sounds very different when amplified through hearing aids. Some tones are muffled, others exaggerated, some are bent enough to make a sharp into a flat, and all are mixed with the background noise which in amplified in excess proportion to the sound you want to hear.

However, lest I sound ungrateful, were it not for the nuisance of hearing aids, I would have suffered much more from life-long hearing challenges. In spite of it, many "deaf" persons have become fine musicians. I was told that I could not become a musician, and certainly not a doctor (you have to hear through a stethoscope), and thanks to God, family, and so many wonderful teachers, I did both. Remember that when people tell you that you can't do something, they are really saying what they could not do. They have no idea what you can do!

Bless Those Hearing Aids!

Yes, hearing aids are a blessing, a nuisance, costly, noisy, store wax in your ears, and other troublesome stuff, but, you see, it's like this: There are lots of tables in the dining room about 5 or so feet apart. They tend to be filled with either all Geezers or all Goozers. That's because most folks in these "residential homes for the aging" are single. Their soul mates, if they ever had one, have gone on to happier hunting grounds. So, they share even the most intimate things with those around them. Most of the folks are to some degree deaf, some to a great degree! So, they talk louder. And there's a rule about this. The louder you talk, the louder they talk to either talk "over you" or they think they cannot be heard. So the law of "exponential volume" takes over and the volume is decibel challenging.

You could see this as a terrible thing, and at times it is. But it also means that those at other tables have free entertainment and are challenged to talk even louder! To others who write books like this, it offers a free ring side seat to collect fodder for writing. Writers like me can turn up their hearing aid and secretly store up the most juicy stuff they think others can't hear. Without hearing aids, this book would never have happened.

"Organ" concerts

For a little levity, let's talk about the "organ" concerts that occur every day. They are certainly not musical! There's the liver, the spleen, the heart, the hemorrhoids, and the inevitable "UTI's." There is an alternate vocabulary for some things. Like the word, "fissures," which is understood to mean that one uses Preparation H. It's amazing how much anatomy Geezers and Goozers know without having the benefit of medical school. They are experts on all of your ailments, not so much on their own, except that they know you are wrong if you try to share your knowledge.

I've already said something about words, but not enough. Many old folks really do try to be proper. So, they avoid noxious language, such as bowel-movements, urination, diarrhea, and others than I'll skip. Common jargon for bodily functions is often used as well, and you know those words well, so I won't repeat them here. Nellie just says, Jill, "did you have a good one today"? Everyone knows what a "good one" is. Much "oldster" medical vocabulary has become outdated now to those in our new medical world, but Geezers and Goozers know the jargon. Everyone should know what "lumbago is, and "the shivers," "the crud," apoplexy," "barrel fever," "consumption," "dropsy," and of course "French pox."

Real music

Let's get back to talking about real music. Music is a phenomenon that cannot be ignored. We hear our first music at about 20 weeks in the womb, and the fetus actually starts to move with the rhythm. The brain begins to retain brain musical sounds and the memory of musical tunes which often stay with us until our last breath. Watching the eyes of a person with dementia light up to a familiar childhood song or loved hymn tune is enough to prove the point.

A friend of mine, a concert pianist, found the Emperor's Concerto (Beethoven) unusually easy to learn, and less a problem than piano literature considered less difficult. She understood why that was so when her mother, also a concert pianist, told her that while she was in gestation, that she, her mother, was incessantly practicing that piece for a performance!

Visiting student recitals, visiting musicians, even the background music in places where the aged live can be calming. Music is healing. It is the language of angels. The problem is that younger generations invariably choose the music which is often cacophonous to the aging ear and a terrorist blast to their hearing aids. Frequently, they say, "whatever happened to 'real' music?"

Learning to play a musical instrument, even in old age, has profound, positive effects on the brain, its retention of logic, function, space, time, and the vibrations of mind/body to earth. Stella at 97 is playing piano beautifully by the way. Even with arthritic hands, the healing of music is seen and felt. There is no culture in the world that does not have music. Nothing could be more beautiful than seeing an aged person sharing their innermost person through music.

It is important to keep music in one's life, regardless of any hindrances. It is still the language that stills troubled hearts, sooths mourning and grief, excites one to action, and brings the right hormones into play. It is truly the international language.

Left-hand turns

A mother of a clinical psychologist friend of mine would not make a left-hand turn when driving. She was fearful when others made left-hand turns. The family tolerated it and, of course, relieved her of driving when they were in the automobile. She became ill with stomach cancer and became unable to drive. As, unfortunately, is most often the case, she suffered for several months in the dying process. In her last moments, when in severe distress, it seemed, according to her psychologist son, that she "wanted to go," but could not do it. He leaned over and said, "Mother, it's safe now, you can make a left-hand turn." He said that she turned her head to the left, took a deep breath, exhaled sharply, and passed away.

Was it the beans?

Lester has no problem reminding you of his "gas" or for that matter, yours. He says that "gas" is a new thing for him, and that he has endured the problem for only 10 or so years. As you get older, what you think happened yesterday really happened a long time ago. Time is irrelevant. The name of any day will do. All days are the same. The "man with gas" insisted that every day was Saturday because he did not have to go to work. He avoids certain foods, but we all agree that he has not found the one (or more) that should be avoided. His dining buddy insists that he change the socially unacceptable word "gas" for "flatulence," but Lester says you should call it what it is. He says that the odor does not bother him so why should it others, and he says that substitute words do not adequately describe his problem. All agree that changing his vocabulary will not change the aroma or auditory nature of his surroundings!

It's all in what you hear

Lorita kept insisting that she was not thirsty when her husband only wanted to know what she wanted to do on Thursday. And he kept telling her that she could go to the potty and get her own cornflakes. Come on, be kind. Pantry and potty do sound something alike, especially if you are from Boston. Sheila was in trouble with Cliff when he asked her for another piece of *toast*, and she kept trying to get him to understand that they did not have *roast*. Then he accused her of not being a good *host*, to which she replied, "Yes, that's right, you have been that way for the *most* of your life." To which he said, "I never lived on the *coast*"!

False teeth or dentures?

I'll never forget Goozer Elsie, (wanna bet? I forget everything). A lovely lady with such ill-fitting dentures. We always called them "false-teeth," but dentures sound better and cost more. Her dentures probably once upon a time fit, but bodies change as it ages. Bones crumble, flesh deteriorate, and muscles turn in to bags of fat. Faces that were full and non-wrinkled, are now more like old purses made from raisons. Such infirmities only exaggerate the problems of loose-fitting false teeth. I still like the term "false" for "dentures," since they are indeed false, and do not do anything close to what the sophisticated term "denture" would imply.

But then, once you get over the clackity-clack of those talking with their false teeth, it isn't so bad. No, that's not entirely true. You might get caught sitting at the same dinner table with Elsie. Then, oh then! Food gets in the way of the clacking, and, talking with a mouthful of food simultaneously being masticated by false (meaning less-than-true), teeth become a real hindrance to one's appetite. False teeth attempting to escape from a moving mouth with mashed potatoes and partially chewed beef is not a pretty sight.

Advice, wanted or not

One thing of which there is no dearth is advice. Remember, Geezers and Goozers alike are incredible encyclopedic resources, and of course, have an insatiable need to share their wisdom. They should be given a great deal of credit for knowing the answer to your question before you ask it. Then, if their answer doesn't fit your question, the topic of conversation is abruptly changed.

On Clifford's first day at his new home in a retirement village, he, and his wife, had lunch with Barry and Linda, his wife, who had lived there for several years. They, as yet, did not know each other's names, but were friendly and seemed compatible. Clifford, said to his new-found friend, "My name is Clifford, what is yours?," to which Barry, without the slightest hesitation said, "You need a haircut! I'll tell you a good barber." Although Barry did not need a haircut because he was bald, he had no reluctance to let others know when they did. And Clifford learned early on that advice does not have to be sought out! In old folks' homes, Geezers give it freely and without hesitation.

It was Muriel who insisted that Lila cut the toe out her Italian-designer shoes to accommodate a hammer toe. And Finnie found that vinegar will solve nearly all of your digestive problems and tells you before you ask. Lisle says that Brylcreem hair pomade works well with his comb-over, and strongly suggested that other balding men try it. Jerry insists that Vicks VapoRub foot massage nightly prevents colds and sore throats. Jay believed that a little drenched in well-salted butter makes even the worst cabbage a better dish.

Gary knew from sad experience that one rest room was 64 steps from the dining room and the real "men's room" was 89, so he was always dashing to number 64! He usually made it there. The greatest advice-giver though was Walter, who "discovered" by unsolicited advice from Alvin, that if you sit in the wrong chair at lunch, "you have taken my place, please move." Walter thought that kind of seat "ownership" was only found in older denominational churches.

MARCH

"I talk to myself a lot because I need expert advice."
—LAWRENCE, P.

MARCH IS A PRETTY monotonous month for most seniors, except for Easter, that is, if it comes early. No holidays, only hum-drum birthday parties, and variations in the weather. Except when the world came apart with Covid-19.

Pandemic or pandemonium?

The year was 2021, and the days of Covid-19 were serious, confusing, dangerous, scary, and particularly anxiety provoking among the elderly. Only a few, talk about the really big "elephant in the room," but we all know what it is very well. We are old, we all have co-morbidity issues, most are to some degree immune-suppressed. We may very well die soon; sooner than we had anticipated. Every day at this, or any, age is an extra gift, so to spend it in isolation, unable to see our spouses who are in healthcare, unable to enjoy a meal with friends, and unable to see our families, is a kind of torture we certainly never envisioned. Depression, discouragement, suicidal thoughts, and mental anguish become part of the diagnosis.

When Covid-19, the flu, whooping cough, or other communicable diseases ae present, everyone is wearing a mask. You seldom meet anyone who even greets you because we know that to open one's mouth is either you give or get the virus, or both! Everyone's afraid of the virus, and other bugs, and rightly so. You don't touch anything at all if you can avoid it, not even the elevator button, and certainly not your outside doorknob (you insert the key and turn it). You're not paranoid, just scared to death. TV, your doctor, the residence staff, and even your neighbors are like strangers ready to pounce upon you since you don't know who they are with that mask on. Bank tellers now give money to people who don't attempt a hold-up, just wear a mask to demand money.

Meals are delivered to your room. They are ok, but even with the highest level of commitment, food tastes good only for so long after it is prepared. Microwaved warmed over food challenges one's appetite. Staff in hazmat type garb take your temperature, which gives you the assurance (possibly falsely so) that you are not at that moment ill. You have become a voluntary resident in solitary confinement, and are rapidly developing your-own mental disorder, (hand-washing – although necessary) known as obsessive-compulsive disorder as well as anergia! Many who do not have spouses are literally in solitary confinement. More than a few, who have luckily survived, have developed signs of serious depression and others a massive case of denial. Some have succumbed to co-morbid conditions and wish they could die.

Spiritual distrust has reached an all-time high, i.e., "Why is God doing this to me?" Many have lost weight, some live all day in sleepwear, others sit and look at the wall. A few have found ways to keep from going crazy. I'm one; I write! We all ask, "Is this really how we are going to have to spend the last days, weeks, or maybe even years of our life?"

Note; This story is actually not a fictional story; it is more like a journal entry, and did not have to be included. But it did, because this book may be seen by someone in years to come who will need to know why grandma did not come to visit, and others will know why they could not visit her.

Signs of love continue

Every story reminds me of another. I just can't tell them all. But I can tell you about Muriel and Tom. I'm just not sure it is really completely true. I know events like this happen; I've seen them, just not this one. Sometimes it is hard to tell if I remember a story or the story of a story.

Muriel said, "Tom, you don't stroke my hand like you used to, and I miss that." To which, he leaned over his rocking chair arm and gently stroked her hand. She said, "Oh Tom, that feels so good. But you don't rub your beard stubble against my cheek like you used to either." He rubbed her cheek with his stubble. "Oh Tom, that feels so good. But, you don't nibble my earlobe and whisper sweet nothings in my ear like you used to." He got up and went into the house. Muriel got up and ran after him, apologizing and saying, "I'm sorry Tom, I didn't mean to make you mad." He smiled and said, "You didn't make me mad. I came into the house to get my false teeth!"

Hobbies

The importance of hobbies is not stressed enough. Particularly for both Geezers and Goozers who have worked at a singular job for a lifetime and have not acquired anything to take the place of that when they retire. They plan on taking up golf, for instance, only to find that their back and knees no longer support that sport. Others say they will play bridge, and that is sometimes possible for a while, until they cannot remember what cards they hold, or which move their partner just made. Others say, "I'll read." And many do, but again, only until their glaucoma or other vision problems blossom. It seems that their arms are not long enough to see the words, and they swear that books and papers use smaller print! But, until these things happen, hobbies are very important and allow a transition from a brain well occupied to one that is rusting in soliloquy.

Many older men aren't ready to give up their woodworking hobbies. Which is really good, that is until reflexes slow down and machinery becomes dangerous. They fix the old ladies' antique and broken cane bottom chairs, and save the administration tons of money by volunteering to make and fix bookshelves, etc. Of course, administration must be very circumspect, since some of them know more than those on the payroll about construction, repair, and remodeling. Competent competition is very threatening to the younger and insecure! Keeping the expert knowledge of the inhabitants in line is a touchy thing. You see, they are often caught between the wish to get out of work that a resident might do and the need to keep that resident from thinking they are needed.

It's mine!

Jerry decided to undertake cleaning up the woodworking shop that had been the sole domain of a single inhabitant, who upon moving into the facility had essentially donated most of the equipment. Now, giving" stuff to a place where you live and use it every day, takes on a special kind of meaning. It is no longer "yours," but then, after all, it isn't quite all "theirs" either. And although it is still "yours," it is at the same time "everybody's." The woodshop is a new kind of senior's "sandbox" and carries with it a unique definition of "my toys."

It all sounds so fair, until after a tool is broken, one asks, "Since it is yours, are you going to pay to have it fixed?" The answer is, of course, "No, it now belongs to the shop." It doesn't happen often, because, in truth, most residents are really respectful of each other. But then, if "he's using my tool and I need it right now, what do I say?," or, "Who took my drill out of the shop and did not bring it back?," or, "No, I really can't believe he loaned my wrench set to his kid that doesn't even live here; he believes it is still his! Ownership is a hard thing to give up. Many things that become of little or no value in reality are things that only years of hard work earned.

Is Cleanliness still next to Godliness?

I need to get on with Jerry's attempt to clean up the shop. It gets cold in Chicago, where he lives, and the shop is not attached to the main building. The heating system (there is no cooling system) is antiquated at best. The vacuum system is plugged up from wood dust, mice houses, and general debris. The original "manager" had never cleaned it to any degree. An inch or so of wood shavings on the floor is a hazard to walking. But I must admit that the cedar shavings smelled really good. The wood-dust on top of the light fixtures effectively eclipsed the light, and the wood scraps in the furnace room were certainly a serious fire-hazard. At least they did not allow smoking, which would have added another dimension to the dangers. Or, for that matter, has anyone heard of spontaneous combustion. It's not unknown in woodshops.

But that's not the most interesting thing. Have you ever seriously undertaken a study of "jerry-rigging "? Electrical cords, and jerry-rigged equipment are interesting combinations of non-psychiatric shock treatment machines, deranged meat-slicer appliances, and fire hazards. In one shop there were bare wires stuck into wall outlets, and motors with belts held together by homemade wire clips. These folks long ago proved the endless use of duct tape! It goes on and on.

The inevitable answer when confronted, "It worked in my shop for years!" Things that work on springs are apt to attack you when you least expect. And, for heaven's sake don't remove a wooden wedge from under anything – it is not possible to know what domino chain reaction it might encourage. If you haven't guessed, things like this is why good administrators don't allow the in-mates to manage the asylum!

He didn't remember from kindergarten

Geezers and Goozers are usually too old to remember anything from kindergarten, and in truth, most did not have kindergarten when they were of such an age. Henry did not go to kindergarten.

But, for those who did, a major rule, as Robert Fulghum reminds us (*Everything I Need to Know I Learned in Kindergarten*), is "put things back where you found them." But remember, if it's mine, why can't I leave it out. I'm going to use it again tomorrow. Community living can be a difficult transition for many. It is sometimes extremely stressful for "only children." It is amazing how many single children or not, have not learned the rules of sharing and respect for persons. Someone has said that the elderly enter a second life of childhood. It is easy to believe.

Measure twice – cut once

My grandfather and several uncles were fine woodworkers. Grandpa Johnson built many huge, beautiful mansions in downstate Illinois. They had solid wood baseboards, perfectly carved crown-molding, hand-nailed oak wood floors, and winding staircases with fancy hand-carved newel posts. Everything was "hand-made." There were no electric tools. They drilled into me, "measure twice and cut once." I learned that lesson both from hearing it over and over, and, the hard way, more times than I'd like to admit. Wood was expensive and cutting and carving all "by hand" was arduous. Careful thinking in the shop was believed to carry over into a more frugal and productive life; and it did.

Bill's error

Then there was Bill. A life-long fine woodworker with impeccable skills and a houseful of personally crafted fine solid cherry furniture. I keep thinking of him because my grandfather was such a person. As I said, he repeated over and over, "measure twice, cut once." Good advice indeed. I'm sure Bill knew this rule, but something went haywire. He made a very fine dovetailed box, for the eventual ashes of himself and his wife, in two very discreet and well-crafted compartments. All was well until he died. Somehow, he had not measured twice or was mistaken twice.

The box was too large by ¼" to fit the columbarium. Other craftsmen, had to, rather unceremoniously, take the box apart and cut it down to fit. There was a lot of gossip about this, and questions about where Bill (his ashes) was during reconstruction. If possible, Bill has some answering to do, when and if he is met "up there." He'll be questioned about his demand for other's perfection in the light of his goof.

Mexican food

Larry, and his wife Nellie, were wonderfully bright and accomplished persons. Both held doctorates from prestigious universities. So devoted was he, that he could be seen trudging across campus in the coldest of weather, in his bathrobe and slippers, to fetch morning coffee for his seemingly unappreciative bride. It was hard to know whether to be proud of his devotion or see him as an indentured servant (most thought him to be the latter). Larry's wife, Nellie, was vocal, very vocal. One evening, Nellie at dinner seemed to be on a warpath; not that such was all that unusual. Her war-cries were well rehearsed. It seemed that she did not like Mexican food. Of course, the waiter had nothing to do with the menu offerings. But that didn't matter to her. He was Mexican, so surely there must be some connection between "always having Mexican food on the menu" and his ethnicity.

Humberto, the waiter, was a model gentleman. Everyone at the table was embarrassed. Knowing Spanish (which was unnecessary since he spoke beautiful English), others gave him an apology in Spanish, which for which he gestured a wink as a 'gracias'. After her tirade about hating Mexican food, and not being the least bit sorry or embarrassed, she then proceeded to order the Mexican entree! Catharsis comes in various ways. She found many ways to spew hers.

For fair and righteous retaliation, she was informed by others at the table that such behavior was not only unnecessary but totally unappreciated. She could care less and her behavior remained unchanged. She proved that you can't teach old dogs new tricks, or Geezers or Goozers either!

APRIL

"I'm tired of waiting for other people to make me happy,
so just get out of my way"
— VELMA S.

APRIL IS A BEAUTIFUL month most anyplace in the United States. When Easter is late, since Easter is a "moveable feast," it can be in March or April. Folks in the mid-west and north always like it in April when the weather is better. The air smells fresh and the earth begins to give up the hibernations of winter. Birds perform their mating calls, and tiny creatures are seen flying and crawling. Flowers are blooming, leaves are turning green again, and the robins sing. This environmental energy is felt in everyone, especially seniors. Some have been shut in due to weather and can now be outside. Some are lucky and have windows that permit the sun to shine in their rooms for the first time in several months. Spring is nearly always felt as a time for renewal.

Some are able to sit on the patio, underneath large umbrellas and enjoy the sun, and others sit on the porch during the rain showers. Many love to hear the birds sing and can even name them. Everyone likes to watch and sometimes feed the squirrels. April, for many, is a breath of fresh air.

Double-dipping

Amidst the beauty of spring, there is a down-side to the month of April; it is tax time. Tax month is not fun for anyone, but especially for seniors. Seniors have paid, and paid, and paid. Geezers and Goozers are right. They paid taxes when they earned it, they paid taxes again on everything they have ever bought, and now pay taxes again, on what they have already paid taxes on! Many must also pay to have someone else prepare their tax forms, since they are not mentally able to do so. No, April is not a fun month for every senior. It's a time when the government you thought loved you really doesn't care about your hardships.

Seniors, for the most part, are generous. All older folks have reconciled that "they can't take it with them." Most have arranged their wills, looked at charitable organizations for gift-giving (sometimes not careful enough), and many are generous with their children and their church. The part that organizations do not understand, ministers included, is that this is the second time many seniors have dipped into their finances for giving. Many were faithful in tithing and gift giving in their wage-earning years, and now they are dipping again into the savings from those same funds.

"I might need it"

Psychologists tell us that what we don't have as children, we often attempt to make up for later in life. Living in the work-laden generations of the past, and depression-days, sometimes barely surviving without enough money, and sometimes not much food, some elders hoard. Most do not realize that they are "hoarding." They see it as keeping what they need or may need in the future. Many see it as collecting, but-in-reality, they don't selectively collect, they keep everything, because "you'll never know when you might need it." The dictum is, "if you want to know if you need it, throw it away!"

Geezers have suits, "collected" in their closets with 1950's wide lapels, ties half as wide as their shirts, and trousers with 2" cuffs. They have fine leather-sole Florsheim Imperial, two-tone, winged toe shoes, that some even keep polished. They may be old, but not "worn out." At one time the trouser waist and shirt collar fit, but aging makes unbelievable body changes. But then, you never know when you'll need that suit, so keep it. Now to be fair, some only keep one good one to be buried in, but then only to be disappointed, since they will be cremated, and a suit is rather unnecessary.

Goozers sport the kind of lace that label them as 19th century holdovers, and some insist on wearing spike heels intended for young ladies willing to torture their feet. Men who want to keep peace do not count the number of shoes his spouse may have. Leland, however, has been known to refer to Beula as Imelda! But to be fair, some wear slacks with sneakers, and don't care what others think. They will tell you that they are saving their "good shoes" and fancy dresses for special occasions. Women dream of more "special" occasions than do men. Goozers in old folk's homes create special occasions and revel in dressing up.

The Geezers usually hate special occasions and make up every known excuse to be an absentee on such occasions. As much as the widowers miss their deceased female partners, they find a sort of blessing in not having to constantly invent excuses to get out of "dressing up."

Nobody Wants It

Some have kept beautiful collections of dinnerware, jewelry, figurines, etc. and display them. It is hard to give up things that mean a lot. Younger people do not know what it means to work hard to buy something, only in later life have to give it up. We spend the first half of our lives "collecting," and the last half "getting rid of." Material things can carry great sentimentality and meaning, and Goozers and Geezers can't understand what they call our current "throw-away" society.

A major disappointment comes to many when they discover that "times have changed," and their solid cherry furniture, and beautiful dinnerware is no longer appreciated. They are saddened to find that many of their children think that the sterling silver table-ware only has the current going price of the metal. Most homes for the aging routinely refuse gifts of fine grand pianos, since they have all they can use, and to be fair, many younger folks just don't have room in their down-sized homes and apartments. Plus, the fact that with employment mobility, the cost of moving furniture, particularly a grand piano, is very expensive.

Durability of furniture is less important than being able to pick up and move easily, re-outfitting with cheap plastic. It is very sad to see furnishings you saved for, and loved, to be given to the Goodwill, Salvation Army, or other charitable organization. Fortunately, some offspring cherish family "pieces" and happily enjoy inheriting them. Affluence, mobility, and a more pleasure-seeking population has no doubt brought much sadness to many Geezers and Goozers.

Depression is real

Melvyn was prone to depression. Psychologists, psychiatrists, his minister, and a myriad of others had through the years attempted to allay his unfounded fears, dislodge his delusional phobias, and extricate him from his self-manufactured anxiety. All with no success. However, at last he found peace at 88, when he saw life ebbing away. Someone has said that most cases are settled on the courthouse steps. As he, and many others, approach the end, things of a spiritual nature take on previously ignored meaning. Melvyn found solace with the chaplain who helped him to re-visit his early childhood memories of a Godly grandmother, who sang the old hymns while she worked around the house. Childhood memories of love and caring, returned to him the assurance of hope. It's never too late to collect on the good things in life.

Lest those who have never experienced true depression, rest assured it is real. The brain simply does not secrete enough serotonin and "happy hormones" to counteract the painful disappointments in life. Persons who are depressed often do not know that they are depressed. They only know that their world "has fallen in on them." Aging is a prime breeding ground for depression. Life's regrets, loneliness, fear, illness, and a loss of hope burden many aging minds. Psychotherapy, pastoral counseling, and often psychotropic medication is required. Many older folks resist mental health counseling because "they are not crazy." Many are not offered that help because they are seen as "getting old" and are not recognized as needing help. Family members and friends need to be alert and help.

Dementia – the slow brain death

Alzheimer's disease, and other dementias are not nice things. They rob the mind like peeling off one layer of an onion at a time until there is nothing left. It is painful to watch. Those who have it seem to know it is developing, but those in it suffer less than those who must care for them. In tragedy there is humor. Shakespeare was the master at mixing tragedy and humor. Many things that folks do when suffering from dementia are actually quite humorous. And, if in their non-demented mind, they would laugh along with us.

A dear lady suffering from multi-infarct dementia once insisted her purse had been stolen. Nothing where we lived had ever been stolen to our knowledge. As it was, two workers had been repairing a light fixture in the closet where she always "hid" her purse, and it was missing.

The apartment was searched for it with no success. Her daughter searched for it with no success either. Her son, who knew "we'd just overlooked it," also searched – with no success. So, not wanting to do so, it had to report to administration. And, although they knew of nothing ever being stolen, they asked if they could search, to which permission was given. And no surprise – they also had no success. As a result, they had to report the loss as being "missing, possibly stolen" and notify the electrical contractor of the incident.

Many months went by. A new purse was purchased and the old one forgotten. As is often the case with older ladies' purses, not much was in it anyway, except a compact for make-up, an out-of-date driver's license, and a few coins. The most valuable item was a folder with pictures of the grandkids.

One day, upon arriving back home after an errand, she exclaimed, "to her husband, you'll never guess where those guys put my purse!" She found it. Where? On the back side of the lazy-Susan in the corner cabinet in the kitchen, the only place no one had looked. But then, the next week someone put her necklace in the refrigerator!

The Voluntary Prisoner

Everyone at Hillside will always remember Flavius. He was bright, a very bright professional in the medical world. No one knew if he'd always been "different," just eccentric, or a bit "off his hinges." At this point he was at least an embarrassment more than once to his friends. He was known to dress in a prison jump suit, that he claimed was authentic, although he claimed to never have been in prison. It looked very real. He had the leg chains and handcuffs to go with it. No one knew where he got them, government issue or clandestine purchase, or. . . whatever.

Believe it or not, he wore them more than once to dinner and scared the living daylights out of some of the Goozers. The story is told, and known to be true, that he was once a guest at a party and showed up at a local restaurant in his prison garb. The restaurant owner corroborated the story. It took all they could do to keep the *maître de* from calling the police.

Microwave Excitement

Then there was Hubert, who just couldn't remember how to use the microwave. On the other hand, maybe he did remember, but just had a different use for it. He stored his pots and pans in it and one day forgot and turned it on! A mighty explosion and fire resulted, which was tragic but thankfully, no was injured. Furthermore, he provided the most excitement the place had seen in many a day. I think for reasons no one could verify, not long after that, he was mysteriously moved to assisted living.

His microwave wasn't the only thing he forgot how to use. He had found that everything can be stored in the refrigerator, including his car keys! Hiding his wallet behind books seemed more intelligent but then he couldn't remember which book was the grand guardian. He spoke often of missing his kitchen for cooking! He was soon forced to give up driving, so the problem of lost keys was once and for all solved. But then, where was his billfold? No, you are wrong, it was not in the refrigerator. It was found, several days after he complained of its loss, by the housekeeper while watering plants, in the Peace Lily flowerpot!

Just can't stop writing

Leona was the Goozer model of "Once a writer, always a writer." I herewith accuse and pardon myself. I understand that old writers never die, they just keep erasing! Catharsis comes in various ways. Writing is one of the best ways. A claim to fame is a hard thing to give up, so why bother? At least, that seemed to be what Leona thought. She wrote, and wrote, and wrote!

Poems, stories, articles, and memos. She had volumes hidden in the anterooms of her mind that could be pulled up for use at a moment's notice. In all fairness, some were funny, others ridiculous, and most were of value to those who had nothing more to do than read useless verbiage. She was a reporter, journalist, writer, historian, and storyteller, all in one.

Of course, it didn't take that much material for most elders, since one page can last a long time. After reading it several times to remember what it said, then you must go back and remember what it was that you were reading. Wordmongers are important though, even though her meager audience slept through her poetry and "readings."

Ruby was another writer, actually of some renown. She was an absolute warehouse full of stories and something of a "walking encyclopedia." You'd think that a person with that store of knowledge would garner tons of friends who would surround her with bated breath to hear the stories. But not so, you see, being smarter than others doesn't pay off. Smart is like yesterday's left-over cabbage casserole. You just don't need it anymore in these establishments, plus most of it is like hardened sour cream icing on a dried-out lemon cake. The problem was that writing was about Ruby's only claim to fame, and certainly her only remaining skill. Bathing others daily with her knowledge, however, did not bring her friends or happiness.

To be honest though, true to journalistic ethics, don't always make for good stories. So, just like this book, a little is added here and a bit there. So often reporters, of course, only see and hear what they see and hear; and it's often not the "whole" story. You can't write about a half-story, so somehow you have "find" the "rest of the story." Paul Harvey was the epitome of that kind of "finder."

MAY

*"I love to plant flowers, but since I can't get back up,
I end up planted too"*
—*LULU Y.*

MAY IS FOR MOST parts of the country a beautiful month. It is the month of flowers, Mother's Day, graduations, and bursting into summer. But for older folks, May is not always that beautiful. Their own mothers are long since gone, their children are often scattered, and some, believe it or not, pay little or no attention to them It seems that the older generation has more sentimentality. They can no longer plant their flowers, they cannot tend to a garden, and their grandkids are graduating from schools and universities. They helped with the tuition, of their kindness. Health issues, mobility, travel restrictions, and yes, sometimes money, are real hindrances.

Gratitude is in the eye (and nose) of the beholder

There is so much for which to be thankful. You'd think old folks would be grateful, and for the most part they are. But in some instances, such is not the case. Martha's kids showed up and as they sat with her, they noticed that she was a bit uneasy and slipped off into a near nap every few minutes. But each time she fell to the side, the attentive staff would slip a pillow under that side and prop her back up. Of course, then in only minutes, she'd fall to the other

34

side, at which time again the staff, wishing to make a good impression on the relatives, would stuff another pillow under that side. The daughter, remarked, "They certainly are attentive and kind to you. You barely fall to one side, and they are right there to put a pillow under you and prop you back up." To which, Martha said, "Yes, but it sure does make it hard to pass gas!"

The growth of girth

Herbert's problem is far from unique. Over the years he has nurtured a sizeable and still growing midsection. So much so that he cannot now bend over enough to even see his shoes, little alone tie them. That wouldn't be so bad except that he is under doctor's orders to wear compression hose every day. They are tough enough for a versatile, slender person to get on, but nearly impossible for Herbert. So, of course, he requires help. We all felt sorry for poor Mary, the nursing attendant, who is assigned to assist him. She literally has to bury herself under that enormous adipose growth to get to his feet. At which time, she complains that the odor is anesthetizing and is constantly augmented by additional wafts of less than pure air. She has suggested that he should just wear the sox 24/7 and save the "home" the potential workman's compensation.

His-giene is not always hygiene

It is no polite or politically correct to refer to overweight persons as being "heavy," or almost any other term. The real effect of this is a kind of denial that helps no one. It is a deception that everyone, including the overweight person, know is simply not true. The older generation is not so touchy and owns up to such problems much easier than younger folks. They have grown up in an era where truth was more important that political correctness,

Ralph is such a person. He is no small boy at about 5'10 and 320 pounds. He takes offense when people try to "beat around the bush about my weight." He makes it perfectly clear, "I am fat, very fat, and the correct word is obese. As a matter of fact, my doctor admits as well that I am morbidly obese. Which means that my weight is a death sentence." He admits that he can no longer see take proper hygienic care of himself, and all who have olfactory senses know that to be true.

If anyone thinks that workers who endure, and mostly with a pleasant attitude, taking care of this kind of human disgust are overpaid, need to re-think for sure. Further, the humility to which one must admit, that it could one day "be me," is staggering. It's not only obesity, but that combined with arthritis, memory deficits, and no spouse or family to execute orders, the end result is tragic. It becomes the duty of those poorly paid, but devoted caretakers to attempt remedial action.

Ralph has taken it to heart and has begun walking (shuffling) daily, watching his diet, and working on his mental attitude. He rightly states that he eats out of frustration and loneliness, having put on over 100 pounds in the three years since his wife passed away. Ralph says, "when you can't see your shoes, let alone lean over to tie them, it's time to get on with "getting it right before it kills me."

Let there be light

Some things are funny beyond words. Cecil lost his cell phone. Now, few of that age bother with cell phones, but Cecil is unusual. Having a history of education and employment in the technology industry, he prides himself on keeping up to date. And, by and large he does so. He owns and uses a computer as well, and, is usually very much "with it." But he lost his cell phone and was hunting it feverishly, only for Maynard to notice that he was wandering around in the dark using the flashlight on his cell phone to find his cell phone. When confronted with the obvious, Cecil, being the erudite professor emeritus that he is, simply said, well, "How could I find it without light in this dark room?"

Logic is not necessarily validation

Raymond prided himself on being "logical." But you see, logic has its limits. The most essential limit being the degree to which it validates or confuses. When it validates, it does not have to make sense, only to sound academically logical with paradoxes, incorrect metaphors, or even neologisms. When it does not validate, it is obviously misunderstood, based on out-of-date information, or otherwise obtuse and of no value, hence disregarded. Age has its benefits for not being confronted for inconsistencies or correctness, since all recognize that a defense for saving face is far more important than much else.

Old information is seen as valid due to its ability to withstand the onslaughts of time, kind of like Louis, the Geezer, whose knowledge was impeccable although rarely accurate. His wife, the Goozer lady Jessica, who was actually much smarter, but wise enough to say very little, attempted to correct him. That was always a mistake. She tried to be logical, but it frequently brought down his wrath, and whipped up way too much support, for her among her other Goozers. So, he spewed his knowledge to the few Goozers that would listen.

Logic is useless when one lives by the outdated paradigm of corporate management, as did Raymond (who, by the way, was too pseudo-sophisticated to be called "Ray"). He maintains that logic is only for those who cannot understand reason!

Reason is no match for a Cadillac

Wesley was undoubtedly one of the most difficult with whom to reason. He drove a car, or rather, the car drove him. He had owned a Seville Cadillac for many years, always trading it in each year for the latest version with all the latest gadgets. He lived in a cottage in this fine Florida "Sunset Village," which was slightly less than a block from the main building where he had to go for dining.

He was a bachelor who prided himself on saying that he'd never had any time for women. He gave much advice to his fellow

37

Geezers who had married and could do little about it now. But they would listen as he spewed on, "they cost money, all they want is more clothes, more parties, and they just yak, yak, and yak." Funny, but those without wives sitting close enough to hear often agreed.

Now a block was entirely too far to walk for a gent like this, who has been pampered by wealth and well-paid servants, so he drove. Or, as you've guessed, has his car take him (he saw his car as a servant, as he does most things and people). He was slightly less than 5 feet tall, and when hunkered down in the driver's seat under the steering wheel, he actually looked more like Kilroy looking over the fence. Comical but very dangerous. It turned out to be more dangerous for his Cadillac which devoured the garage door while destroying itself. A brand-new Cadillac had no more brains than his previous one and suffered multiple fractures when barely off the showroom floor. In the state where he lived, driver's licenses were basically automatically renewed for 5 years, so the last known, at 97 he had five years yet to go!

No medical training required

As a physician, I have the not-too-often appreciated need to diagnose. No, of course, I don't tell non-patients my diagnosis, but I find that most residents have the same skill without medical training. It's called "observation" and "personal experience." Or sometimes intuition, or just a wild guess. A yellow stain in the right place is not hard to diagnose. A brown spot, likewise. Then there are the multiple decorations of pie, gravy, and coffee that adorn the bosom of every so well-endowed Goozer!

Some Geezers have resorted to bibs which look a bit odd but so very sensible. A chunk of chocolate just at the side of a Goozer's mouth says a lot. So does the smell of a bit too much Jack Daniels or Coors (alcohol). Although smoking is prohibited in most homes for aging, it seems some of the Geezers are known to sneak in a stogie from time to time. Some Geezers, and Goozers too, do their best to disguise their signs of aging, but it rarely works.

Glenda proudly announces, "I paint my toenails red, so nobody knows I've got toenail fungus"! Merlin responds by saying, "That's why I still dye my hair so no one will know it is nearly white." Good, now no one knows!

Then there's Lawrence who admits that his "figure assisting" elastic undergarments is right down painful, but he pays the price, and his buddies laugh as they see him stretching and pulling from time to time trying to untwist certain parts that must be turning gangrenous!

But, as any well-trained medic knows, a diagnosis is only as good as the availability and knowledge of treatment. And for most of the ills they try to hide, there is no treatment. And, for folks with so little to talk about, maybe its good for them to have a few not too dangerous physical problems to commiserate with each other.

Wilhelm's birthday party

There's Wilhelm who was blessed with a group of both Geezers and Goozers who gave him one great, bashing, birthday party. They all gathered in the dining room around the 6-foot round table, with the seldom used but much appreciated white tablecloth, and the huge German chocolate cake, with some kind of gooey, chocolate icing and a candle for every ten years. Since he was 80 that made 8 candles, all aflame waiting for him to make a wish a blow them out. However, all-of -the sudden, a waiter tripped, sending his platter of dishes on the floor behind Wilhelm's party.

Of course, it forced everybody to look, including Wilhelm, who when he abruptly turned fell face first into the cake with the burning candles. Fortunately, the gooey icing came to the rescue and extinguished the candles! There was, however, nothing to do about his new haberdashery adorned with German chocolate cake. The chocolate goo on his glasses, and the bits of hardened wax among his singed hair and mustache was hilarious, for everyone except Wilhelm. Everyone laughed but Wilhelm. Incidents like this are really quite good for the old folks though, since it tends to build some much-delayed humility.

JUNE

"I was born in June, and I was married in June. My husband died in June. I hope I survive this June."

—MARIE D.

JUNE IS A MONTH full of special days. Weddings, Father's Day, and a rapid entry into summer. Like Mother's Day (the 2nd Sunday in May), Father's Day has come to mean very little. Mother's Day still has at least a tinge of importance, although none of the Goozers and Geezers still have living parents, some of their kids do, but even many of them don't worry about special days. Their fathers have all passed away; only the memories remain. Many of the older generation hardly knew their fathers, since they were born in the days following the Great Depression (1929) and their fathers were working two or more jobs, just to keep food on the table. They were without fathers during their adolescence since most of their dads were off to WWII. Then just as they moved into young adulthood, their fathers (and many of them) were off to the Korean War, or Vietnam. Some were luckier. Most were not.

Some think that their mothers (or fathers) don't know them anyway or are so "out of it" that their presence doesn't matter. They forget two things: many folks that look "out of it" are not, and they are most ungrateful to not remember those who forget them. Some mothers receive flowers and some get cards, and some have never been mothers. Special days take on a very different meaning for folks who often feel slightly less than incarcerated in a place they do not want to be. But to be fair, some are treated with appropriate flair and attention, and are shown true appreciation and love. June in past years, more so than today, was the month for weddings. Many seniors were married in June. Mine was June 25, 1948! Few still have living spouses hence, June can be lonely, sad, and feel very empty.

Language arts

Language sometimes suffers in places like this. Not all have the same polished vocabulary. As a matter of fact, even those who do, in their later years, often revert to earlier expressions for emphasis. Older people can get by with being a bit more seedy in language sometimes, it seems. Some seem to enjoy breaking out of their "proper" language and showing that they have an acquaintance with vulgarity.

Most places for the aging are amalgams of ethnicities, cultures, religions, and "acceptable" language. The "red-neck" good ol' boy Geezer has a different idea about what can be said in public, than the prim and proper Goozer from the far up Northeast around Harvard.

Victor's language, who came from somewhere in the backwoods, was known to be a bit more colorful most of the time. After all, he had served a lifetime in the navy, driven 18 wheelers, and rode a motorcycle. Agnes had gone to have her annual medical check-up. He was listening attentively to Agnes recite her wonderful doctor's visit. She reported that he had done a thorough "head to toe" examination and declared her "totally fit and in good health." When she finished, he calmly but sarcastically asked her, "What did he say about your fat ass?" To which she calmly replied, "He didn't ask about you!"

Copy-prone

When people assemble in groups of similar persons, they invariably become imitative. Watch it. You'll see it. John sits in a rocker and starts to rock. David is sitting in a rocker but not rocking. Within seconds he will start to rock. Bill is mumbling while he trims his fingernails with his pocketknife. Within seconds Gary will dig out his pocketknife and start trimming his nails. Stand and look at the sky – looking at nothing. Watch and see how many others will immediately start staring at the empty sky!

Sometimes consciously, but mostly unconsciously, we all imitate. In "homes for the aging," many arrive standing erect and walking without a cane. They are obviously in good health and have no need to slump, stoop, or shuffle. Soon they begin to take on the posture and stance of those around them. At first, they just bend their head to hear the bent over walking partner. Then they begin to bend to meet that person's level. Soon, they are bending enough to also need a cane. Now they are almost twins in posture. Before long, they are both able to hear and walk together in sync as they wheel their rollators.

Where is Cecil?

Talking much too loudly in the dining hall, but without any or adequate hearing aids, Jolene and Ruby thought they were having a private, very private conversation, but they were not!

Ruby: Jolene, did you have a good one this morning?

Jolene: Uh, no, not very good.

Ruby: Maybe you need to take more Metamucil.

Jolene: Oh, that's great. Where did you meet Cecil?

Ruby: I didn't say that I met Cecil. I said to take more Metamucil.

Jolene: I thought Cecil died several years ago, he was such a good man.

Ruby: I didn't say Cecil, I said Metamucil.

Jolene: That's so nice, please tell him hello for me if you see him again.

Ruby: Jolene, turn up your hearing aid!

Ever-emerging contraptions for mobility

The immobility of past generations is rapidly changing for the better. All kinds of moving contraptions for hallways, roadways, stairways, and even public transportation has evolved. The equipment for living in these places for the aging, therefore, is also rapidly changing. Only a few years ago, unstable folks just held on to chairs, or carefully moved from one place to another. Now the inventions of wheels on walkers, and the ubiquitous motor contraptions make life much easier. Some of them are in the Rolls Royce range, while others are more like an entry level Ford. But they have bells, lights, four-wheel brakes, windshields, flag extensions 5 or more feet tall, and everyone awaits an announcement of personal television and GPS equipment.

The latter might not be a bad idea, since many do in fact get lost on the way home (one block away). If the local constabulary were to look carefully, they would put speed governors on them. Oh, and they could also use mechanisms to see stop signs, since such are either ignored, or seen as gentle suggestions, by most of their oblivious operators. Like children's chairs in kindergarten, the vehicle signs are not standard street height but lower to be seen by the many who struggle with arthritis and other diminutive skeletal problems.

Art, the local NASCAR Aficionado

There's the true story of Art who had been a race-car driver and had his rig painted up in NASCAR "officianata" stipes and numbers. It is not exactly known just how he souped up his road non-legal vehicle, but it could, and did, outrun all other competitors. The "road laws" at his home for the aging in Minnesota, are perhaps a bit more lenient than elsewhere. He could make it to dinner faster than anyone else. The problem was the pond in the middle of the campus. In the northern regions of the US there is such a thing as sleet and ice. Art had not equipped his four-wheeler with "winter tires" or "snow chains," and the road around the pond, really could not care less. The ice got its way, and the fearless NASCAR envier lost his grip and his vehicle.

Only his ego, and possibly his billfold was bruised. They could have left his contraption in the pond as a reminder to others, or a monument to stupidity, or a future underwater fish sanctuary, but alas, they removed it. It seems that soon after that he qualified for an upward mobility event, sans vehicle – to assisted living.

Mobile Carrier Meets The Elevator

Virtually all elevators will now accommodate wheelchairs, mobile devices, and other equipment of that nature. Unfortunately, neither the elevator nor the mobile contraption has eyes and the ability to operate without a human. And there is the problem. Aging eyes, slow reaction time, memory of what button has been pushed, and the location of wheels, legs, and other attached appendages can be a problem. Mary Ellen is a very sweet and considerate lady. She would not offend anyone. Her hearing is severely impaired, and her eyesight, as estimated from the thickness of her glasses, is approaching 20/200! "Mary L" as she is known, is 89 years young, she is sharp, and polite. But her oversized wheelchair does not seem to share those abilities.

Her problem, or I should say the problem for other people, is that the over-sized rubber tires on her mobile device get stuck on the side of the elevator door, prohibiting the door from either opening further or closing. When the automatic eye in the elevator senses that something is "in the road," it attempts to close, but it can't since the rubber tire refuses to let go. So it alternatively jerks spasmodically between trying to open and close. Jim, her husband, a bit less feeble, but surely not as smart, decides to help. He bends over between the wheelchair tire and the elevator door in several vain attempts to extricate it.

In the process, he loses his hearing aid, in the crack between the elevator floor and the elevator shaft. In more vain attempts to find his hearing aid, which of course is not going to happen, while working on the tire, he gets his hand stuck between the tire and the door.

Now you understand, there are others in the elevator. They all realize that this situation is going to take considerable time to resolve. Julie tries to squeeze out the door but gets her purse caught on the arm of the wheelchair. Her body is now out of the elevator (mostly) but her purse is not. So Jim tries to get Julie's purse off the wheelchair arm, while temporarily giving up and looking for his hearing aid, and letting the rubber tire grind to itself. He gets his hand free, but it is bleeding (he is on blood-thinners) and the sight is not pretty. Furthermore, Julie is very distressed to see that he is getting blood on her Michael Kors handbag.

Julie is starting to choke and says that blood makes her sick and that she is about to vomit. Kenneth came running from the other maintenance room but forgot his beeper and went to the wrong elevator, only to call the office and say that he sees no problem!

Randy has his legs crossed and seems appropriately impatient, hoping for a resolution "in time." The only other person aboard is Karl who gives "expert" advice about how he handled a problem many years ago when he was stuck between floors in New York.

The correct maintenance folks arrive and the entertainment continues. They are quickly able to disable the elevator's automatic brain but are very reluctant to do anything about the spurting blood from Jim's hand. George warns them of liability if they hurt someone. He says he knows because he had once started law school but dropped out after one semester. They call the nurse. They are also able to quickly get the wheelchair tire unhitched from the door, except in the process, "Mary L" now has a wounded husband and a flat tire. At this point, Henry, it is reliably reported, left the scene and the end of this saga is unknown.

Your keys don't fit this elevator

Merlin really wasn't trying to use his keys to operate the elevator, but in his moment of absent-mindedness, he dropped them, and for the once in a thousand chances they fell between the door of the elevator and the floor when it opened! Down the shaft they went as those waiting with him heard him give praise to the Almighty! No problem, the next day the ever-gracious maintenance crew, with great pomp and enjoyment, climbed to the bottom of the shaft and retrieved the keys. Often the "problems" of the elderly are grist for a bit of joy for those who so faithfully, and great respect serve those whose minds and bodies fail them!

Weighty matters not-to-be taken lightly

Obesity, as has been earlier stated, is a common malady, not only among the elderly. Much levity has been given to persons who suffer from this problem. And, that is shameful. But it is so much more problematic when one's knees and other load-bearing joints decide to retire from service. Hip replacements are common, and so are failed joint surgeries. In truth, the surgery did not fail, the new man-made joint, is no more capable of abuse than God's first gift. The world of the over-weight elder is serious. Hip and knee replacements are now common even in later life. Fortunately, many seniors are being more careful not to put on weight in the event they need such a replacement, but also many seriously lose pounds and fair much better after getting a new hip or knee. The blessing of regaining mobility has transformed the world of aging.

On the light-hearted side, you can almost hear the chair begging for help when the bulging flesh pushes its arms beyond original design, and the architecture of the table is not intended for elbows supporting more pounds than the table-legs can bear. It is not humorous and is not "nice" to think in this way, but, the physical infirmities that accompany a life of obesity are too numerous to ignore. The problems often resulting from being overweight affect more than just the bearer of those pounds. Other persons and accommodations suffer as well.

The person with the weight suffers the most. Irreversible diabetes, high blood-pressure, kidney and liver failure, and the inevitable earlier death, force one to at least consider the ramifications of obesity. To consider over-weight as "normal" and "natural" is not helpful. To blame say it is "inherited," or "it's just in my DNA," makes for good talk, but does nothing to alleviate the results of the problem.

To be critical, is to be politically improper and socially uncouth, but not to be attentive to at least one's own proclivities in this department, is to be self-destructive. There is no adroit, politically correct, way to deal with this problem. Kindness must prevail, and admit, that like others with physical afflictions, "there but for the grace of God go I."

Keep moving

As they say, "use it or lose it." This is really true. Many an older person finds out that when they attempt to regain a lost skill, even balance and motion, that it has "got up and gone." Regular maintenance is the key. Staying occupied while one departs from this life is a real challenge. Wellness staff personnel do their dead-level best to help.

Brittle bones, arthritic joints, deteriorating muscles, hearts only operating on a couple of cylinders, and an energy supply that's just about out of gas, make it a tough proposition for the resident and "wellness-coach" alike. Chair volleyball, table games, and limited stretching is helpful. Board games, puzzles, and large print books are also good, but they, like Bingo, are no substitute for bodily exercise. The best defense against body atrophy is physical activity.

Many seniors fight boredom. This is a particularly difficult problem for those who also have mobility limitations, but many find productive ways to outwit it, which is wonderful. George crochets shawls for shut-ins, Mary knits booties for the new-born at the local hospital, Melody cooks at the local food-kitchen, Melba does repair sewing for residents. Bill restores donated furniture. Gerald paints and donates his paintings for charitable causes. Others find many ways to avoid boredom, while unfortunately others seem content to complain.

Uh, What's Your Name?

Eldon has been a psychiatrist for his entire career life. He is a proud graduate of a top 10 medical school, and a respected Fellow of many professional organizations. He is 93 and prides himself on his memory, and, in truth it is impressive. He is forgetting names, though like most folks much younger. He also forgets faces and mixes up folks. He blames this on failing eyesight due to macular degeneration, which is probably true. He has a great line, "I don't forget much, but I always remember that I forgot it."

When the memory fails, the excuses old folks make for not remembering are often funny, obvious, and sometimes just ridiculous. John, when he can't remember a name, asks, "Excuse me, I'm sorry but I forgot your name," to which the listener says, "My name is Kevin," to which the speaker says, "Oh I remember that, but what is your last name." If the listener gives a last name, the speaker says, "Oh I remember that; what is your first name"!

Health issues Aplenty

Jeremy says that his chaplain told him that his soul is well, but he complains that his hip joints are sick. Mary Ann, complains that her nose runs and her feet smell, and she thinks that's the opposite of what it should be. Kenneth, the retired optician, says that his eyesight no longer allows foresight, hindsight, or insight, and he can't imagine how bad it will be with any other kind of sight if he goes blind. Joe says that the pain in his neck somehow got better right after Nelda, his wife, died! Jean says the podiatrist said that her "highfalutin" pointed toe shoes caused her hammertoe, but she wears them anyway.

Weldon insists that sitting on cold and wet logs to eat lunch while working in a Minnesota lumber camp, caused his hemorrhoids, even though his doctor disagrees. Then there's Sheldon who walked the steel beams in high-rise construction, who insists that causes him now to be "deathly afraid" of heights. Lewis won't walk around the lake because he may encounter a snake, and he grew up where there were many and was once bitten by one. Josephine, says that she loves her long, bejeweled earrings, but they make too much noise in hearing aid.

JULY

*"You'd better believe I'm a fire-cracker,
I was born on the 4th of July."*
—HAROLD F.

JULY, AMONG MOST SENIORS, is remembered as a big vacation month. The road trips, days of fishing, time at the beach, up to the mountains, or spending time in the summer cottage. Some still own their cottage but are unable to visit it anymore. Most cottages are not built with sufficient safety features and often have many outside steps, and only upstairs bedrooms. Further, most can no longer enjoy their boats, tennis clubs, golf, and other physical activities. Travel is out of the question. For those who are fortunate, July can be a beautiful month for travel and vacations. Others must stay home and play Bingo!

I didn't say that!

A collection of happenings in Bingo at five different retirement communities will make you laugh. And, they are real. Louise, bless her heart, tries so hard. But her hearing impairment makes only for more entertainment than winning the game. The caller yells out "22" and she wants to know where we "are going to." Then Gene hears "44" and hollers out, "what's it for." Then good old retired high school principal Lloyd hears, "88" and says, "no, I don't want anything more, I just ate." Rosa insisted that the caller kept talking about what they were "fit for," but he was really just calling out "fifty-four." The incredulous one was Alice who kept getting upset every time the caller yelled out, "sixty-six." She kept saying, "I wish you'd stop talking about sex."

It reminded me of the minister who said, "This evening we are not going to have a sermon. The message will be in our songs. I'm going to yell out a word and I want you to tell me a song about that word, we will then sing it." He then hollered out, "Amazing," to which everyone cried out, "Amazing Grace." He then said, "Love', to which Elmo yelled out "Love Lifted Me." He then said, "Sex," to which elderly Thelma, in a creaked voice yelled out, "Precious Memories." I think after that the preacher gave up. Probably not a true story, suppose?

It is not nice to be rude, however, some of these folks, particularly the older men, in a widow dominated environment, that only have rudeness as their winning tool. Some could be decent friends, if the pursuer only wanted that.

Mourning and grief are not the same

Mourning usually continues for months, sometimes much longer, but is not consciously distinguished from grief. Conscious mourning slowly resolves into grief, which in some persons never resolves. Mourning tends to be more of a physical thing. In some cultures, they wear black armbands or other evidences of being in the process of mourning, for prescribed periods of time, with specific rituals to be observed during that period of mourning. However, grief tends to exude more slowly, from the inner person, the soul, and continues to produce stress and dysfunction for unlimited periods of time.

There is no culture which prescribes a time-period for grief. Both conditions can develop into the "broken heart syndrome." Others become chronic disablers for any kind of normal life. Some are sufficiently severe to cause the patient to allow the inner spirit to die and sometimes take the physical body with it.

Tears are sacred

Tears are precious and shedding them is one of the greatest medicines for the soul. The Bible is explicit in its sacred regard for tears (Psalm 56:8; Rev. 21:4) The Scriptures speak of saving tears in a bottle. Psalm 56:8 in the Old Testament refers to God who collects our tears and saves them in a bottle, indicating that God pays attention to our pain and suffering and considers tears to be evidence of that pain, thus sacred to God. As-Sinjari wrote that weeping for devout Muslins is a means by which to reach Paradise. Weeping was a sacred ritual in the Medieval West, and the Tapirapé Brazilians saved tears with which to bathe each other. The sacred nature tears is ubiquitous in all religions, the world over.

There is scientific evidence that the shedding of tears releases oxytocin and endorphins which help to resolve stress, mourning, grief, and pain. Sarah needed to cry and let the tears relieve her soul.

Education and training are absent

Few persons, including the administrative staff in hospitals, and homes for the aging, do sufficiently understand mourning and grief, which is disabling. Most persons do not think of mourning and grief as long-term conditions. They tend to think of them as being temporary; that is, until they personally experience it. Degree programs and training organizations give very little thought to the management and treatment of mourning and grief. Even seminaries for ministers say little about it.

The Western way of death has thrived on the denial of death, and the attempt to make death beautiful, with corpses looking "like they are just asleep," and multi-thousand-dollar funerals, with expensive caskets buried in the ground. With cremation now an option for many, there is a gradual awakening to the reality of death, the loss, the loneliness, and often the physical, financial, and spiritual burdens left to others. Those left behind must frequently struggle on their own, to find a new life, while digging out of the pain of mourning and grief.

Evidence to the ever-present problem of grief, is the number of books that are in print on the subject. *Good Grief*, a small book by Granger Westberg in 1962 (Augsburg/Fortress) is still in print and reportedly selling briskly. There are many psychotherapists who limit their practice to patients suffering from grief. Pastors, priests and rabbis are also often most helpful in working through the process of grief.

It's Amazing, They Know My Name

Julie was absolutely tickled pink when she got a phone call from a certain publishing outfit and told she'd won a brand-new Mercedes and five million dollars. They told her that she had the lucky number, and she just knew that this new technology had caught up with her and that's how they knew her whereabouts and how to contact her. She was about to send in the "fifty-dollar confirmation" check when some good Goozer neighbor convinced her of the scam. She did not send the money, but to this day she is not convinced it was a scam and thinks that she missed the windfall of a lifetime.

A Barber Is Needed

It was the first day in a retirement community and the two couples did not know each other, as a matter of fact, they did not even know each other's names. The hostess simply sat them together at a table for four. The two ladies introduced themselves then Sam , the newcomer introduced himself by simply saying, "My name is Sam," to which the male host person at the table responded, "You need a haircut!" Somewhat taken aback by such a quick and unusual response, Sam, the witty man he was looked at his host, who was as bald as a billiard ball and replied, "Yes, I always do. I wear my hair long. Don' you wish you could?"

Remembered for life

Mary Jane was 10 years old when Gerald pastored the little church she attended. He was in that parish for 8 years and had been gone for over 60 years. She was just another kid in the church to Gerald and gave her no extra attention that he could remember. Nonetheless, she wrote a handwritten letter every month to Pastor Gerald and his wife. After over 60 years Gerald still receives a handwritten letter, never less than two sheets of paper written on both sides, with all the information, news, gossip and obituaries of parishioners. Gerald is now in his 90's and knows none of the names or persons she talks about. Gerald is only one of many to whom she ministers with her handwritten missives. The parishioners he remembers are all but a precious few deceased or moved away from that parish. She knows that, but it doesn't stop her mission for keeping him informed. Her handwriting has now deteriorated to the point that soon her letters will no longer be legible to the postal carrier. No one can read her handwriting now in the letters. But, out of gratitude, Gerald thanks her for her kindness and every few months sends her a small check to cover the postage. The incredible lesson here is the way we touch lives and never know it. How Gerald touched her life, he'll never know, but she does, and she is only an illustration of our touching every day for good or ill.

My Car Key Doesn't Work

Lynn has a spanking new car and so proud of it. The only problem was that Georgette's car is exactly the same color, although a different make. Lynn's car has every bell and whistle available and that means a fob that serves as a key, lock, trunk key, alarm, and much more. Lynn is so relieved that she doesn't have to remember which key is for the car; it's a big black plastic fob. One day she became unbelievably frustrated though when her fob would not work. She struggled and "blessed it out" but the fob simply would not unlock her car. So she called AAA to help her out. They arrived and lo and behold the-key fob would not work for them either. Then astute technician noticed something strange. The fob was for a Ford not a Honda! It worked fine on the correct car. Lynn was embarrassed but happily drove away. By the way, Georgette had a good laugh over it.

Shirley, not Shurley

You'd think that prospective parents might consider the confusion and conusion when they name a child with a bi-generic name. But they don't. There is Kelly, Sydney, Charlie, etc., but then many are sensitive enough to add a letter or two to clarify it, such as Roberta, or attach an additional name such as Ann to make it clearly feminine as Kellyann. But no, Shirley was Shirley and rarely would you meet a more masculine person. He tried spelling it Shurley, but that, of course, did not help. The grief that his name caused him is untold. He recounts being kicked out of the men's bathroom when someone heard (but could not see him in his stall). Mistakenly assigned to the wrong dormitory in college and listed in the women's branch of the U.S. Army! So, he decided to alter the spelling of his name, again to Shurley, but without legally changing it. which did not help. The days of trans=gender confusion arose and he was really in trouble, so he hired an attorney, spent the money, and changed his name to his grandfather's name which was Silas!

AUGUST

"I used to poke my girls in the ribs at weddings and say, 'you're next'. Now they poke me at funerals and say the same thing!"

—JOYCE L.

AUGUST IS FOR MOST folks closest to a "nothing month" as you can get. No holidays, not many weddings, and no buffets! But for those in assisted living, memory care, health care, and hospice, life continues to creep away. One day is like any other, and all stories are heard for the first time (since yesterday), and everyone is a new friend that they meet for the first time (also since yesterday). June said that she thought it must be getting close to Easter because she found a hard-boiled egg on her breakfast tray.

Names are important

Let's lighten up a bit. "Hey George, oh no, that's not your name. I'm so sorry, now I can't remember your name at all." Everyone in the old folk's home has a name. Some do not remember even their own. Others, most older folks, (and many younger) actually remember, the names of only a few.

It is so common that the story is told, (maybe true), of President H. W. Bush when he visited such a home for the aged. As he walked down the hall, he passed an elderly gentleman who was trudging along, oblivious to all including President Bush. So, the

President said, "Hello sir," to which the gentleman did not respond but continued his solidary trudging. So, the President repeated, "Hello sir," in a more exclamatory voice. To which, once again the elder gentleman paid no attention. Finally, the President said, "Sir, do you know who I am?," to which the gentleman replied, "No sir, but if you go to the front desk, they will tell you!"

Perry has the perfect way to deal with not remembering names. He says, "Hello, I'm sorry, I forgot your name," to which the other would answer, "O, that's ok, my name if Jim Short," to which Perry then says, "Oh yeah, I know your name is Jim but I sure did forget your last name!" And, of course, if the other person gives only one name, Perry remembers it but asks for the person's other name.

Western culture is full of folks with unfortunate names. There's "Freida Friday," "Jimmy Job," "Luke Luster," "Ida Bragg," and not to forget "Ima Hogg" (1882–1975). Then, don't forget James Slaughter, MD, the orthopedic surgeon! One of my classmates in medical residency was Dr. Doktor! I like our local dentist whose name was Dr. Payne. Names don't always fit though. Think of the waitress, whose name is "Pleasant," and she surely is not. And, "Precious"; one must wonder who pushed anyone's imagination, but she probably was as a baby – things, and people change! The lady at the cleaners is named Janelle, and her pet dog's name is Bean. Her nickname is Jelly, so, her friends just call her "Jellybean"!

Martha was a hoot the other day. She was frantically running around the grounds looking under every bush and bench. When asked what she was looking for, she said, "I can't find the Easter eggs." Wilmer told her not to worry, that it was not Easter it was Veteran's Day. She said that it had to be Easter because she hid the Easter eggs that morning but couldn't remember where she put them!

Everybody liked George. He wasn't in the least bit vain, and didn't mind what others called him. George didn't care whether you remembered his name or not. He was fine with "hello," "hey you," or most any other salutation. But Joan certainly was not. Her name was not to be confused with Joann, Joanna, Johanna, or any other derivation of the name. And, further, off with the head of anyone who would dare to call her Jo! While, on the other hand, Josephine, a very sophisticated, highly educated, professional lady of national recognition, was just with "Jo" or any other name you would call her, as long as you were her friend.

The wrong name can get you in trouble

Anonymity does have its drawbacks, however. Jay painfully discovered such, when he could not hear the barber correctly, and as a result his head was shaved like Kenneth wanted! And, then in reverse, Kenneth missed his appointment all together because Jay had taken his slot. Merilee was not too happy when the manicurist kept calling her Marilyn. And Rebecca absolutely threw a conniption fit when anyone called her Becky.

The name I have, has shown to have duplicates in every state where I have ever lived (now 7). First name, middle, and last, all spelled exactly the same as mine. I once received an invitation to a high-and mighty ball at a very sophisticated country club. I knew it was not for me, but the name was the same. Without too much research, I found three other persons who could have claimed the invitation, all having the same name, and all living in the same zip code. Amazing but true. Yes, I found the rightful owner, and we had a good laugh. He was of a different ethnicity, and old enough to have been my grandfather.

Now lest I forget, names are sacred too

The Scriptures place great emphasis upon names. Names are unique identifiers, and often unwittingly depict personality. The Old Testament is particularly explicit in the necessity of carrying on the family name through male progeny. Lineage, heritage, genealogy, and other name factors are important enough for whole chapters to be given over to tracing a family name.

The Christian tradition gives great importance to one's name being "written in the Book of Life" (Rev. 21:27), and the importance of Christians praying in the name of Jesus, and baptism in the name of, "the Father, Son, and Holy Ghost." The baptism of a child always emphasizes the child's name. A person's first name, in English-speaking cultures, has traditionally been known as one's "Christian" name.

In many religions, persons acquire a new name for various reasons. Monks are given a Dharma name at ordination. Islamic writer, Ibn al-Qqyyim spoke of the strong relation between a name and one's identity. Under certain circumstances, in Islam it necessary to change a child's name, because it is too heavy and the effects upon the personality will be too great. Chinese culture insists that a child's name is tied luck, and even future education and career. The name of a child in Japanese culture is always tied to a specific meaning, such as, "beloved," "honest," or other attribute.

All religions place great emphasis on a family name, lineage of many generations of the same name, and the importance of sons, for the assurance to carry on that family name. Hebrew names with "Ben" in front of the surname (last name), means "son of," and is highly prized. To bring shame upon the family name in many cultures is a grievous offense. In some cultures, to bring shame upon the family name, is sufficient reason to commit suicide.

On the other hand, it is an honor to greet someone by their name. It bestows identity. It shows respect and even honor. The Nazi regime stripped people of their names and gave them tattoo numbers. Prisoners are not known by their name, but by a number. Patients have been known to be "the appendix case in room 413." Many other illustrations could be given of the tragedy of losing one's name. To lose one's identity changes the very person.

Next time you meet someone, greet them by their name, look them in the eye and see how much it makes a difference. Misspell most any word in a letter to someone if you must, but do not misspell their name! We live in an age when personal identity is being lost to numbers. Being called by a number is reminiscent of the horrible holocaust days. Let us not repeat that ignominious practice of stripping others or ourselves of identity.

Seeking more than is sought

Some, not necessarily younger, but sometimes so, are looking for something more; maybe love, companionship, friendship? Who could blame them? Many are grieving widows and widowers, mostly widows, since men seem to leave for heavenly pursuits, on the average five to seven years, before women. Although with women taking more places in the traditionally "male world," they also endure mechanical accidents, industrial mishaps, and bodily wear and tear, thus are catching up with earlier demise.

Nonetheless, watching those seeking "more" can be an enjoyable pastime. That is, unless you are one of the "being pursued" against your wishes. Games that you have never heard of, and others that are salvaged from childhood and adolescence are fair game. If were not so serious to the seekers, it would be humorous. And, it is, somewhat.

The methods of pursuit are myriad. I suspect that you've not thought of these methods, devious and sometimes down-right overt, since you were much younger. Some of them are notes tucked in your mail slot, birthday cards with "early birthday wishes," or "sorry, I forgot your birthday." Gifts of food that you didn't expect, and often not on your diet.

Then there are the phone calls with obviously made-up reasons for the call, embarrassing looks in public places that cause others to ask you, not them, what's going on? Notes slipped under your door. Interruptions when you are talking with others, with the obvious need to be noticed, but always with, "I'm so sorry to interrupt, but I need. . . . ." And more and more.

It is not nice to be rude, however, some of these folks, particularly the older men, in a widow dominated environment, that only have rudeness as their winning tool. Some could be decent friends, if the pursuer only wanted that.

Loneliness is a disease in these waiting rooms to the afterlife. When one reaches 80, 90 or more years, there are few friends left. Family often lives far away, or if near, they are working with their own active life. Mobility is limited, even though sometimes funds are not, so that they cannot travel to see the few friends and family still in the picture.

CAN I TAKE LESSONS?

Isabelle, or Izzy as she liked to be called, decided it was time to shop for a gift for their soon-to-be-born grandchild. Of all places, she decided to go to Walmart. When questioned why she didn't go to a more up-scale store, she simply said, "I need to save my money, there'll be more grandkids coming." Freeman, her always obedient husband, reluctantly agreed to take her and decided he'd be able to shop for some wax for his car.

Everyone knew that he'd been exceedingly dominated by Izzy for their entire marriage, so he was certainly less than a "free" man, but he didn't seem to mind. While going through the store, Freeman noticed that he'd lost track of his wife and simply looked terrified, since he knew she had memory loss, and might not know where she was or be able to find her way back to the front of the store. Looking a bit forlorn, he was noticed by an older male volunteer worker who asked, "May I help you sir?," to which Freeman said, "I've lost my wife," to which the volunteer smilingly replied, "Can I take lessons"?

Her tears would not stop

Then there was Sarah, the lady that cried for months. It seemed that nothing could stop the flow of tears. Unfortunately, too many attempted to do exactly that. By that, I mean stop her from crying, when what she needed was to cry. Mourning and grief are serious experiences. They are all too often taken lightly but can be deadly. Sarah is a current example in her Florida retirement home.

Her husband of over 56 years passed-away following a recently diagnosed, short 6-week acute bout of, pancreatic cancer. She is in mourning and grief. She is in the throes of lonesome, inner pain. Knowledge of grief will follow later. She has now been a widow for only 12 weeks and has lost considerable weight, is not eating properly, shows signs of negligent body hygiene and only relates to others in a dependent, clinging fashion. She weeps almost constantly and seemingly cannot be consoled.

I have talked about many funny, and several serious, residents, but this one is one of the saddest. There is nothing humorous about it. Her mourning and crying will not be relieved until she allows it to turn into grief, nor should it. Many other cultures have specific mourning rituals and do not deny the emotion of loss. Western culture has been entirely too "macho" and called it "bravery" when it is in fact avoidance and denial.

Yelda took the prize

It is not known for sure whether Yelda ever drove for the Indy, but she may have. She certainly took the prize for speed, rapid U-turns, making zero-turns, and running over things not intended to be run over. Her real claim to fame locally was taking the prize for the most "hit and runs." Now, most would say, "hit and run *accidents,*" but she did not see them as *accidents* at all. They were very well calculated *incidents.* Her 4-wheeler horn put the Model T honker to shame. Actually, she had two – and some residents expected that she would soon add a high-powered, air-horn like on 18 wheelers. If she honked her horn(s), and the object or person in the road did not move, it was obviously not her fault if her carriage plowed into it. With all the humor this story might generate, there were indeed some sad happenings, one of which ended up in the hospital with a broken ankle. Everyone, brave or strong, feared the would-be demolition-derby driver.

SEPTEMBER

"My forgetter has gotten so good that it's hard to remember what I've forgot!"

—AUDREY S.

THE KIDS GO BACK to school, the days are cooler, and the holidays are "just around the corner." Some have already started digging through their storage bins for Christmas decorations. Halloween is coming soon too, as well as Thanksgiving. Even though greatly diminished from earlier life, many make the most of the season.

Jake, the dog and bird lover

I've mentioned the problem of hoarding. But The Melody Home had another problem related to it. They had a resident who liked animals; a lot of them; all at one time, in the same house. One pet, maybe two, is common and usually not a problem. At least, as long as the owner is able to take them outside for walks and bodily needs, and if they don't yip or bark incessantly. However, when a person like Jake loves so many it can be a serious problem.

At one point he had 14 dogs, and 10 birds. They were "sneaked" into his villa home. He'd never have gotten by with that had he lived in one of the central apartments. He loved them like children, which is probably fine, except that, in-spite-of his refusal to take them outside, he did not have "indoor accommodations" for his dogs. Nor did he believe in caging his beautiful birds.

He was known to ask visitors to please not return (although he did not have to), when they objected to the waste from his dogs and birds, the odor, or for that matter when a dog decided to use the pantleg of the visitor for a fire-hydrant. Of course, since the dogs had never been outside, they would not know that fire-hydrants exist. It is of truth that upon his separation from that facility, many thousands of dollars were required to gut and totally remodel his unit. Disgusting enough for one story?

Fences

Someone has said that fences make good neighbors. That seems like a strange statement since good neighbors have good relationships, and fences don't build relationships. However, most homes for old people have fences. It's kind of like cemeteries; no one wants in and no one who is in can get out. Now, once folks move in, most residents don't worry about leaving. Most residents in retirement homes plan for that to be their last "home." Most of the 42" fences could easily be traversed by a child, and there are no man-eating animals attempting to devour the aged, crippled, bits of protein that shuffles around inside the fence. Some fences are attractive, but in truth, most fences only prove to further the institutional look of such places.

When administrators are asked, "Why the fence?," the inevitable answer is, "security." The outside world is hardly at danger from the residents, and those with any intent to enter would see a fence of less hindrance than a sign, "No Trespassing." Fences and signs are like padlocks, mainly for honest folks. It's an identity thing, kind of like putting your arms around yourself to claim ownership, I guess. They say fences make good neighbors, but no one there is looking for neighbors, and a wrought iron fence hardly keeps out even the rodents.

But administration likes the look for public relations and marketing purposes. They also claim that it helps with their liability insurance. The residents don't know why they should pay for a fence they don't like, but they pay for lots of things they don't like. Furthermore, like any corporate body can be expected to do, it's administrators pass the buck, and simply say, the decision was made by the "higher-ups."

Ambidexterity

Pete is a dear older gentleman who spent his life devoted to people's eyes. He was a celebrated ophthalmologist whose recreation was napping. When someone claims he was napping, he simply answered, "I was very carefully inspecting the inside of my eyelids, you should try it." He had some other idiosyncrasies however, that were a bit more troubling. He's probably the only person known, to pick his nose with the forefinger of his left hand, while attempting to clean his right ear with his right pinky. I must admit that he was quite successful with both as the evidence on his fingers proved.

Emergencies can be fun

The nature of emergencies, in houses for the overtime of life, are always highly secretive. It may be the recently deceased resident passing in the hallway, with all doors closed, and everyone peeking out any crack possible at the body-bag on the stretcher, trying to guess who it is. Or, everyone is gossiping, wondering, "Ok, who now burned their toast and set off the fire alarm." To which all residents "must" retire to their pre-designated station and await the "all clear." Of course, few go anywhere, except to gawk out the window at the welcome excitement.

It's very disturbing, when the event is on the other side of the building from your room, and you are not invited over to see out of your across-the-hall neighbor's window. Those few who follow instructions and retreat to their assigned "safety zone" can be found wandering the halls, after the "all clear," trying to find out from anyone what happened. Most do not go to their assigned "safe zone" out of obedience, but because the fire alarm sirens are deafening, the strobe-light flashers are blinding, dog's yelp with pain, hearing aids are jerked out, and within seconds everyone is brain dead if they don't get out of their room.

In truth, many have become quite adept at diagnosing the nature of the "emergency." You see, if it is health-related, the fire-truck, paramedics, and often another emergency vehicle arrives. If only a fire alarm, it's better than nothing on a dull day, but you only get to see a couple firetrucks. Everyone knows there is likely no fire, and therefore, no reason to guess who is going to be moving from their apartment. It's just a matter of time to blame someone, rather than thank them for the excitement.

Size matters

Sometimes names are just too appropriate, like Bertha. Bertha came from a wealthy, dignified family from the Northeast and had taken a large, luxury apartment in a western Colorado, mountain view "Village." This is a serious question: Are you making fun of a person, if you laugh at something they do, which to most seem funny? Of course, most things are funny only if they happen to someone else.

We all do, I think. In this case, having the name Bertha didn't help. She even laughs at her own name in relation to her size. Bless her heart, according to her, she has always been "large." That's not the problem. Nor is it a problem for anyone that knows her. And there is no evidence that it has ever been a problem for her. She is simply loved by all. So, we can put any idea of "largeness" out of our minds.

Well, until word had it that she met a dreadful fate, at least according to rumor. Bertha sat down a bit too hard, and the dining room chair cried out in pain as a leg broke, leaving Bertha smack-dab on the floor, with the broken chair on top of her. She laughed harder than anyone else. It's so gratifying to see people laugh at themselves. She even offered to pay for the chair. She never really understood that it wasn't the furniture's fault, but that wood and metal just can't win over weight and girth!

This story continues in rumor. In places for the elderly, one can never fully trust a rumor. When it turns into gossip, it then has the validation, even if incorrect, of a larger, therefore more trusted body of believers. Once gossip has passed the gossip test, it is absolutely true. So, since it is still rumor, not gossip, this story may or may not be true.

The Figure does count

Geraldine was a beautiful woman, with what has come to be labeled a "full figure." The crisis came one day, when for reasons no one will ever find out, she simply could not extricate herself from a given plumbing fixture necessary for certain bodily functions. Rumor and gossip, has it, and, oh on good authority, that housekeeping made every attempt to solve the problem, only to have to ask maintenance to give a hand. It seems that the seat of that fixture had to be removed first from the fixture with the occupant "in place," then removed from the occupant by some special means! Needless to say, much secrecy and lots of gossip, accompanied this event. She did seem to be aware that several folks looked at her with a quizzical stare.

Obviously, with help, she won the battle, since she showed up, totally in her New York style interpersonal control, at dining that evening, acting as if nothing unusual had happened. Every little old Goozer tried to get an invitation to her apartment for any reason. Of course, they would need to use the un-named convenience, so that they could possibly verify any damage resultant therefrom. To my knowledge, no Goozer succeeded. Geezers, of course, only made many not-so-nice jokes with this fodder.

It's not just about women

It seems that most "jokes" regarding physique, etc. are about women. The truth is that it should be quite otherwise. It's just that men don't seem to talk about it as much, and women are more discreet, leading men to take advantage of the situations.

It was known on good authority, that Wallace, a widower living in Pennsylvania, sported a mid-section of tremendous girth, and a derriere considerably larger. He enjoyed soaking in the bathtub, until he realized that flesh and water, when in contact with porcelain, can produce a powerful vacuum. He could not extricate himself to get out of the bathtub. The helpful maintenance staff, with smirks on their faces, completed the job. They said the bathtub let out a huge sucking sound when the vacuum let loose. Towels, a bedsheet, and his bathrobe made the sight partially tolerable to those who assisted. Again, on good authority, it is reported that following that incident he resorted to showers!

OCTOBER

"Everything on my body may have fallen, but I'm still a work of art!"

—JILL M.

Don't breathe on me!

HOUSTON HOUSE HAD A couple of retired dentists in the place, but it seemed along with his own dentist, orthodontist, periodontist, and several other oral professionals, including the local otolaryngologist, they simply could not tame down Dan's halitosis. He had successfully invented social distancing long before Covid-19 thought of it. That was bad enough, but his hearing deficit complicated matters. People who are deaf think that everyone is, so they shout. When they shout and have halitosis, it's like an industrial size fan is spray-painting you with fumes.

Dan, the poor guy, really did try to deal with it, but he often said, "I've had it so long, I don't notice it anymore." He was often assured that others were not so oblivious. It would have served as anesthetic for most any surgical procedure. He joked about it saying, "It's like the old saying about the face, 'I know my face is the ugliest by far, but I'm behind it. It's the people in front that get the jar!" Then, of course, in as much kindness as could be mustered, all agreed that "halitosis is better than no breath at all."

Ablutions and the body shop

The folks at Geremany Lake Home take the cake for stories about personal ablutions. How do you properly apply lipstick when you can't see? All over your face, but then, since you can't see, you don't know it until Lilly, who can't hear, but can see, tells you. But then, it is Heather, who can't hear but can see, that finds out from her hearing aid specialist that the silver item in her ear is not her hearing aid, but a suppository, and she remembers where she put her hearing aid!

Don't forget Valerie who complained that she hadn't seen her feet in 20 years. Wilma said she should get new glasses and Valerie carefully understood it had nothing to do with seeing but in her girth and the modern disuse of corsets! Vernon, just said, well, "I have some problems with seeing that far too, and it's a lot more than toenails that I have to deal with"!

Lisle said that his brother's false teeth are now too big for his mouth. As we age, our bodies do shrink, so the facial muscles probably do too. At any rate, he tells of watching Griffin, his brother, push, shove, gag, and then give up trying to put in his false teeth, only then to try sliding them in with KY Jelly. Lisle said it was quite a mess and did not work. He suggested that Griffin just "gum it" until he could get better fitting dentures, but Lisle would have nothing of being seen in public with no teeth. Eventually, he persuaded Lisle to assist him. Lisle says that was quite a circus, but after considerable torture to Griffin's lips, and Lisle's fingers, they got them in, only for Griffin to complain that it felt like a piece of Lisle's fingernail had broken off and was lodged just behind his eye tooth!

No more holidays?

It was almost the Fourth of July, but the stores were already starting to fill up with Halloween, Thanksgiving and even some Christmas decorations. This was very confusing to both Geezers and Goozers, since it's hard for most of them to know what day of the week it is, let alone what holiday is coming up soon. Some of the Geezers thought we should skip them all and make up a new one and call it "Halthanchristhan" Day! Wilhem liked the "Germanic" sound of that mouthful. They thought the new day should outlaw gifts but keep the buffets. Then, they had second thoughts, that they would be losing too many buffets if they discontinued all the other holidays. Convoluted thinking makes great entertainment.

Holidays are less than festive in homes for folks slowly dying in place. The small artificial Christmas tree sitting in the corner on a hospital-style end-table, with one of grandma's antique, but yellowed lace tablecloths, a few sputtering lights and a couple strands of homemade trimmings, just doesn't do it.

It seems like such an impotent attempt to make something real, that no longer has much meaning, to most who sit in their memory deficient minds, and try to make believe they are happy. Jane said, "I just wish they'd let us enjoy our memories and stop trying to fool us into thinking it's all so great." Joyce just wanted another cup of holiday punch hoping there might be a bit of "happy juice" in it. She was disappointed, by the way. Rita was enjoying her fourth caramel-filled Brach's chocolate. Leland complained of the "cramps" after eating five generously iced pretzels with sprinkles. Thelma was still nursing her first cup of punch, with the carefully poised diamond pinky on her right hand, while casting accusing looks at the "gluttons."

Halloween for those still able to be at all mobile is always more fun. They could, with total permission, dress up silly, act crazy (which isn't hard at that age), and eat their weight in candy. Remember those yellow and white candy teeth? But then, Pete says that there's no better lunch than a couple Snickers bars. Some of the ladies have saved hats for generations, and admittedly, some are not only ornate, but beautiful, and nice to see.

False faces are quite a distraction, but often quite clever. Masks may be funny, but they further obscure sight, and accompanying costumes can impair hearing, and make a faltering gait a dangerous shuffle. Fun can turn into tragedy real fast in such circumstances. One wrong turn, or one mistaken sound, all too often becomes a dangerous hip-breaking fall.

It was Rodney Dangerfield who said, "there's just no respect." No one in today's world understands that quip more than seniors. Most were raised in a time when, "Yes, sir," "No, sir," "thank you," "excuse me, please," and other respectful terms were not only commonplace, but automatic and expected - and appreciated. Such is no longer the case. Elders, at least in the United States, are often seen as unnecessary and useless baggage. Younger generations do not see a need to pay any greater respect to the aging than to any other group, and they pay very little respect to any group.

The parts don't always make a whole

Gestalt psychology maintains that "the whole is greater than the sum of its parts." I can assure you that Geezers and Goozers have put that to the ultimate test! The whole world is becoming more gray; wrinkles are replacing smooth skin, and the majority of society is more and more indebted to artificial joints, organ transplants, and other medical engineering wonders.

Wonderful advances for a more enjoyable aging process, but often beyond the financial abilities of many. But, alas, there is a limit as to how much "foreign" material the human body can tolerate. Shellie is now 87 and recently married (her third), Manley, who is 92. They seem much in love, but she was overheard telling her inner circle, that it was quite an ordeal to get Manley ready for bed. He puts his hearing aids in a small dish on the dresser, his dentures in a cup on the bathroom counter, his back-brace on the straight chair, his glasses on the bedside table next to his C-pap machine, and his knee brace in the large leather Lazy Boy. Then, what's left of him is helped into bed by Shellie, since she's the young one. She jokes about "putting to bed what's left of him."

Wheelchair use and abuse

Marie seems content to let Hilman take care of her. She rides around in a wheelchair with him pushing her everywhere. Although a most gracious and loving act, Hilman and everyone else is amused that when he is not looking, she rather spritely gets out of the wheelchair and walks around unaided. He does catch her sometimes, so she just gives him that pitiful, but coy look, and with a show of tremendous, excruciating pain, plops back down in the wheelchair. The joke she makes is that "he just pushes me around and talks behind my back."

Many persons hardly find anything funny about their required life in a wheelchair! Indeed, they would gladly exchange places with those who do not understand their plight. Madelyn, a virtuoso French Horn player is confined to a motorized wheelchair and requires mechanical assistance to get out of it for personal needs and to retire at night. When students, while not intending harm, "joked" about getting to wheel around, rather to walk the university campus, she gently said, "I'm so glad you can walk. I hope you never have this "privilege.""

How do you get ketchup out of that bottle?

Someone told Floyd that he shouldn't get so exasperated when trying to get ketchup out of the bottle. Roy told him just to tap the neck of the ketchup bottle lightly with the handle of a straight table-knife, and the ketchup would come right out. It did! Floyd was somewhat a muscular brute, and his "tap" broke the bottle top leaving a mess of a nearly full bottle of ketchup on everyone's plate except his, and glass shards in everybody's food. He was, of course, not too happy, but blamed Roy for giving him incorrect information.

Who'd I say that to?

Pauline was sitting obviously admiring Leroy at dinner in the dining hall, when he abruptly said," You are beautiful and a widow. I'm homely but single too. Will you marry me?" To which she quickly said "yes." The next morning Leroy was in real trouble because he remembered asking some lady to marry him but could not remember who it was! He thought it was Pauline but was not sure. So, after considerable thought and with much humility, he called and asked her. She said, "Oh I'm so glad you called because I remember telling some man last night that I'd marry him, but I can't remember who that was"!

More WD-40 needed

The wellness folks are committed and do their best to keep knees, hips and other joints from becoming locked in place. They offer tips, and many of them are very helpful, for assisting with mobility, limberness, etc. Creams, jells, patches, micro-current devices, braces, supports, massages, chiropractic, prescription medicine of every sort, over the counter concoctions, mail-order promises, herbs, homemade concoctions, and much denial, go into the failing anatomy.

Pain is not the only handicap resulting from joint failure. Mobility and meeting one's own daily needs are hindered as well. So many daily tasks that are taken for granted are not possible with joint immobility, such as, combing one's hair, clipping the toenails, reaching into all body parts that need attention, and just getting up out a comfortable chair. Pain plus mobile disability is not an easy existence for many. Particularly for those whose pride and need for privacy have been important. Allowing others, often persons you don't know, into your private life is humiliating.

The hose-wrestler

No one has a good answer for Lillian who must, on a daily basis, argue with, and have a wrestling match with her compression hose. Anyone who has ever worn compression hose knows that putting them on is a major activity. In order to do any good, they must be hard to get on and very uncomfortable to wear. So, she can be heard in the hallway talking to them. Yes, talking to them. Well, I mean making noises to them. The noises are sometimes speckled with "why the . . . won't to go on," or "#*^ if you don't-*&%!'" She somehow always persuades them to obey, although if one looks closely, they get their revenge by further twisting in a spiral fashion, with the heel of one somewhere up the calf of one leg, and the top of the other one at her ankle. She's really a very sophisticated Southern Bell, so this problem must irk the daylights out of her, but she doesn't let on about it in public. She lets her skewed hosiery do the talking, and they do!

Your Windows Can Be Too Clean

Emerson was rightly proud of his bright red Cadillac with white leather interior. He kept is spotless and drove it with the dignity of a hired chauffer. He had at least one bad habit though and that was his daily 'chaw.' He said that he'd chewed tobacco since working in the tobacco fields as a young boy. His teeth showed it too. His wife had put up with the stained clothes and other items that his chaw somehow hit when he missed the spittoon. But that was not often. He prided himself on the accuracy of at least at 15-foot spit to the old brass spittoon in the corner, and admittedly he rarely missed. But when he did, it was a mess. But, nonetheless, he never gave up his chaw. Push came to shove one day though, when his spanking clean red Cadillac with the white interior got the worst of the deal. He spat is chaw without remembering that he'd cleaned his windows to sparkling clear perfection, and didn't notice the window was not down! His spat was now not only covering his face as it rebounded from the impenetrable glass but also staining his white leather seats! The window was washed, his face de-chawed, but the seats would be a reminder of that day for the life of the car!

NOVEMBER

"Something's wrong, I just don't know what it is.
I think I lost me."

—MARGE V.

WINTER IS APPROACHING. FOR many the winter portends much more than just cold weather or the coming of holidays. It is psychologically and physically challenging. Darker days, colder weather, and the upcoming holidays, are reminders that life is short, and days on this terrestrial globe are limited. There is Thanksgiving to look forward to; that is, for those who have family who still visit them. For most, it is just another day, like all others. Alone, the same pain, the same faces, and staff who try to care (and many in fact do), but residents consider their "care" just to be part of their job. Winter means not sitting on the veranda, and "watching" the winter storms on TV while they nap.

The cruel disease

I don't know how to relate Lela's end of life, but I must, so that those who have never witnessed or otherwise understood Alzheimer's disease may do so. With huge numbers of elderly living longer with increased diagnoses of dementia, everyone must come to grips with the severity and cruelty of this disease. One out of every ten persons in the United States has been diagnosed with

Alzheimer's Disease, and the prevalence of it is increasing. And that is only one form of dementia.

Over 14% of persons of 65 years of age have some form of dementia. There is no cure for any known dementia. Dementia is an insidious, slow, disabling, and cruel disease. It robs the brain and throws normal systems of the body into disarray. It forces families into bankruptcy and disrupts loving partners. Watching a person with dementia is like watching an onion being peeled, one layer at a time, until there is nothing left. Persons with dementia look into your eyes and you look into theirs, and neither sees a person.

Lela was happily married to her second husband. Her first had succumbed to heart failure several years earlier. Jerome, now 74 and she only 72 planned to enjoy several years of happiness as they aged. Such was not to be. Alzheimer's symptoms began to appear in Jerome shortly after their marriage. It was assumed that, as usual, that the symptoms would progress slowly and eventually become disabling. That was not the case. His symptoms increased very rapidly and required assisted-living care within only a few months. His deterioration moved quickly, which is not usually the case in kind of dementia.

Lela asked if I would accompany her to the assisted-care unit for a visit to him, which I was glad to do. He had been a casual conversational friend of mine. We had both worked as violin makers earlier in life, which gave us things in common to talk about. When we entered the unit, Jerome was seated on a couch, holding hands with another lady, whom neither of us knew. She was obviously suffering from dementia as well, and, was holding a doll. He arose, greeted us and said, "I'm not sure who you are, but I'd like you to meet my wife and our new baby." I can think of no more devastating story!

There are a million other stories just like it, and worse. Such is the fate of those with dementia. The folks in the general public know of the problem, but few understand its severity and the toll it takes on its prisoners, and on those who, with loving gentleness, become caretakers.

Those with dementia tend to wander. It's as if they are looking for something they cannot find. And it probably is. They are looking for their home that they lived in for years, their spouse who may have passed on, their children who do not live near and do not visit, their favorite things, and in truth, trying to find themselves. There is simply not a way to understand what's going on in the tormented mind of the one who must endure it. It is heartbreaking for those who live to care for them. I know!

The fateful night when I had to (with huge tears running down my face), take my sweet wife, against her will, to assisted care, she was wandering, attempting to leave the building in the cold rain, with only her nightgown on. She was waiting for an airplane to take her to her mother, at other times she thought I was her mother! Talk about emotional pain – I can tell you first-hand.

The memory unit

Steve was a fastidious and incredibly proper person. When multi-infarct dementia began to steal his mind, he required more care than Sarah could give him. He was placed in the "Memory Unit." What that really means is the "lost memory unit." He missed Sarah. And I'm sure she missed him too. She was still of sound mind and remained living in their villa across the campus. Steve was certain that she was living in an adjacent memory-unit room and insisted on bedding down with her.

The consternation among staff, to say nothing of poor Beulah (with whom he wanted to bed) was both humorous and tragic. Violence ensued when the staff insisted that he leave the room which was not his, and the woman he was convinced was his wife. This is only humorous because few realize that his painfully diseased mind actually thinks that she is he is wife.

Needless to say, the only answer was sedation. To lose one's dignity in this fashion is more than one can understand, and more than one should have to endure. Memory units are impossible to manage adequately since no two cases are alike, and the range of disability if so large. In most places, the care is superior and exemplary, the staff is loving and caring, and often even the patient's families do not understand the gravity of the situation.

Everyone feels bad for Helen and Robert. Helen has slowly progressive dementia and can be found wandering, not knowing where she is. She cannot take care of herself, and must live in the assisted-care section of Woodlawn's Care Center. Robert, not without the morbidities of aging, lives nearly a block away in his cottage. Helen is convinced that he is living with another woman and has "sent me away, so I won't know."

Harold's wife is convinced that he is her son. She can no longer differentiate his face, his features, his voice, or anything else to dispel that delusion. She has regressed to an earlier stage in life, and out of deranged neuronal activity has made her husband into her son. Whether her thinking causes her distress is not known, it is known that it burdens him beyond belief, although he is wise enough to see that it is "not her" but a demented person. He doesn't know how to handle it though, when she accuses him of being a "non-caring, ungrateful son."

These, and many other heart-wrenching stories are real. My wife, in her latter stages of dementia, often mistook me for her mother. Barry's wife firmly believes that he is her father. Brenda thinks her husband, who has been dead for 15 years, will be visiting her soon, as soon as he gets back from a business trip to Europe. And on, and on, and on. . . .!

Name That Place

Places for old people have a myriad of names. Most attempt to give the place a name that is a bit uplifting, or at least, neutral. They are called, Villages, Communities, etc., but others try harder with names like "Peaceful Acres." Most just call the place what it is, "Vanderbilt Place," or the Village at Elliston," etc. Then there is the unique one that somehow must have had their tongue in their cheek when they named it, "Sunrise Place." Everyone knew it was really "sunset place."

The home at Fairfield Commons refused to install a fence around the campus. Previously I told you about fences and that they weren't of much use. But Fairfield proved to be different. They had a lady leave the place in the dark of night, a winter night at that. She was somehow able to slip out without tripping the alarm. She unfortunately only got a few feet until she fell into a ravine and remained there for a couple of days until they located her frozen body.

All of this to say that security is a huge issue when we can no longer secure ourselves. Many who choose to remain at home until the end, find that more is required than they understand, before it is required! Being secure is more than feeling secure. Doors that appear safe often are not, rugs to trip over are everywhere, electrical appliances that tip over, shower floors that are slippery, hot water that burns, steps to fall down, no one to hear when they holler for help, and much, much more. The recognition of insecurity is not realized until it is no longer secure.

Hobbies are more than pastimes

John simply does not know what to do. He has no hobbies, his wife passed away several years ago, and they had no children. Until sight robbed him of his driver's license, he acquired fine automobiles and kept them shining in showroom fashion. Now, without his cars, and with only limited sight, he is in a tough place. He can't read, barely sees well enough to feed himself and to care for his physical hygiene. What does one do? Audio books are the answer. He is too proud to let others read to him. For many life-long readers, listening without reading is a difficult transition.

It is so important to develop hobbies when you are younger, and activities that you can retain as long as possible. Jigsaw puzzles, word games, crossword puzzles, and other mind stimulating activities are very beneficial to keep the brain sharp, and to have activities that can be shared, thus building and maintaining as many relationships as possible. However, being able to continue a hobby you enjoy is far more enriching. Of all activities, walking continues to prove to be the best all-over activity for both brain and body. Unfortunately, failing bones and joints frequently limit this activity. The brain that keeps active stays sharp longer.

Happy romance

It is interesting to observe relationships as folks age. Time together, such as in marriage, seems to cement emotions into an outward display, whether intended or not. Someone has said that two people who live together for a lifetime even begin to look like each other. I lived with my wife for 8 days less than 70 years, so I should study our photographs, I guess. Watching couples in retirement homes has given me an insight not gained in the study of psychology for many years.

Edith and Cal were great illustrations of a growing affection for each other. They could be seen nearly every evening walking, hand in hand, on the hiking trail next to their retirement home. When you could see their faces, the sheer love and joy was abundantly evident. Their eyes revealed their bliss. I don't know how long they had been married, but it was for many years, that we knew. There are still some great marriages. It is refreshing to see partners aging with each other and still enjoying each other's presence.

Pseudo-bliss

But then, I guess to balance things out. I encountered Ferris and Jane, who had a different relationship for sure. They were partners in living, unwed to each other, and it was not known as to the length of their relationship. Ferris could be ugly, and often was. Not only to Jane, but to most anyone. His braggadocio was disgusting and boring, but there was never enough feedback from others to keep him from reminding everyone of his stellar education and life experience. He was more than paternalistic to his female companion. He was nasty, talked down to her, and in short, he was just downright mean.

Why one stays with an abusive partner is not understood even by the experts. All anyone could do was to observe and pity Jane. Eventually, although they could not confront Ferris, he soon had no dining partners, and no friends. Maybe without Ferris she would have been homeless, who knows? There have been many variations of the proverbial "sugar-daddy." There are also many "strange" arrangements of partnerships, and marriage agreements. It is also not possible to know what makes somebody else happy.

Memories

What we remember as we age is most interesting. We have always known that as we lose our "sharps," we tend to keep long-term memory more than short-term. When we can't remember why we went into the other room, we vividly remember every detail of our childhood home. There are many important lessons in this observation as regards childhood education.

My dear departed Betty was an inveterate reader. She set lofty goals for herself each year. For instance, one year her goal was to read the major French authors, which she did. Another year it was to read the entire works of Muriel and Ariel Durant, which she did. She kept lists of the books she had read. By the time her eyesight and dementia had robbed her of that enjoyment, she had notebooks filled the names and authors of books she had read.

In the end, she could only remember what she had memorized earlier in life. I should not say "only," but "fortunately" in the end she could remember much. One day, our friend Eldon went to visit her after she was over 80% blind, and in declining physical health as well as multi-infarct dementia. She was sitting in her chair, holding the Bible. Eldon greeted her and asked what she was doing. She said, "I'm reading," and told him exactly what she was reading. She quoted precisely, a verse of Scripture she had memorized many years earlier. Eldon noticed that the Bible she was holding was upside down!

What we teach children and what we learn earlier in life, is still important, when many of our faculties for living have left the body. There are many lessons here for parents, teachers, and society at large. Values inscribed on the heart are not easily erased. Unfortunately, neither is it easy to discard wicked and evil lessons.

Gluttony or what?

I've mentioned a good bit about food. But now I remember, Marvin. His name reminded me of a restaurant in the Ozarks, not far from where he lived, named, "Starvin' Marvin's," where you got enough food to "serve an army." This Marvin, at Shady Acres, had a voracious appetite. The food in most retirement communities is adequate. Some places have distinctly higher quality than others, but most have more than survival food.

The problem is with the size of the portions. Marvin needed a scoop-shovel and wheelbarrow for his helpings. Well, not quite, of course. But he was remarkable, at around 5'7," weighing around 140 pounds nude and soaking wet. A three-egg omelet, a double helping of hash-browns, three biscuits drenched with sausage gravy, three pancakes with butter and syrup, and four extra strips of bacon, two extra sausages, and two cinnamon rolls was a good start for him. He was known to return for fruit, and if available, ice cream and cake or pie.

It's a good thing that many others, particularly ladies watching their "girlish figures," ate "like a canary," or the place would have gone broke. Of course, he also took a Styrofoam carry-out home with him. Since he lived alone, we all wanted to see the inside of his refrigerator. He did not have a wife with whom to share food. Surely some of it surely had changed appearance and smell, rather being eaten. But maybe not, given his appetite!

Happy stomachs make happy campers

Food is an essential item in keeping the troops at ease. Folks who enter homes for the aging expect many things. Some more realistic than others. However, food, health care, and security are the top three everywhere. Administration can change about anything else, but leave these items alone, or face disgruntled residents. Life revolves around meals. You get up and eat breakfast, take a nap, then eat lunch, take another nap, then eat dinner, take another nap that ends in bed.

As I think of food, I remember Luke who was very much like Marvin. He was, however, not a glutton. He just simply always had food to take home. He could not possibly devour the amount of food he carried home daily in Styrofoam. His Geezer friends watched in amazement and not too secretly told each other how much they'd like to take a look in his fridge. They thought maybe he and Marvin were running some kind of a clandestine food service! It had to be overflowing with outdated milk and other dairy products, moldy salads, and long since edible meats and vegetables. Maybe he was underfed as a child and had an inner need to make up for it. Or, maybe he just couldn't take a chance on being hungry, a left-over memory from some camping trip.

Telemarketers

Everyone is besieged by unwanted telemarketers. Unfortunately, many of elderly do not recognize these scammers as being illegitimate. They listen attentively, often buy what they neither need nor want, give out their private credit-card numbers and other identification, and believe they have just gotten the deal of their lifetime. The same is true with mailings.

Some of folks have fun with the telemarketers. Especially many of the Geezers. They tell of "that guy from India with the accent I can't understand, that wants to help me with my "compooter." Or the lady that insists I need a warranty for my aging automobile. Then there's the roofer that tells me I need a new roof on the house I no longer own. The great ones are the ones who are not recorded. You see, you can play them and have fun. Just put down the phone and when you come back say, "Could you repeat that, I had to put down the phone for a minute," or if they just won't shut up and are arrogant and rude, just whistle loudly in the phone, or as a trumpet-player friend of mine does, pick up the trumpet and give them a loud blast! Not nice, but don't mess with old fogies.

Mail-in promises

Francis was sitting on the reception room chair filling out the mail she had just received when I passed by. She was so excited to know that she had just won $50,000 if she would only send $50 for "the processing fee." She was in the process of writing the check! Fortunately, Rollie was able to convince her that it was a scam. More often, than not, there is no one to convince these unsuspecting and trusting souls of the fraud they are about to support. Scammers come in all kinds of clothing, with unmatched sociopathic abilities. Children of parents in such places are wise to take note and try to intervene. Many a child's inheritance has gone to fraudulent scammers.

The holding-cell of ailments

I have trouble dealing with the myriad of physical, environmental, mental, spiritual and other problems that beset the elder community daily. Retirement villages, nursing homes, and the varieties of "homes for the aging" are like a textbook of medicine. They are live laboratories where every known symptom raises its ugly head. Most illnesses are slow growing, disabling but not terminal, and completely re-arrange lifestyles, living schedules, and interpersonal relationships. In "normal" life, one encounters many physical and mental symptoms, but they do not dominate one's day. Not so in homes for the aging. They not only dominate the day, but they also become the major focus of life 24/7.

The principal activity for many elders is the management of medications, doctor's appointments, and trying to deny and avoid as much pain as possible. Marital partners become caretakers which vastly changes their relationship. Financial matters come into a different kind of focus due to the incredible prices of some medications. Medications often simply exchange one symptom for another, not always a better one. Compliance in taking medication, is not a matter of willingness, it is also a matter of memory. Since some do not remember whether they took their medicine, they take it again. . .not usually a good thing. They forget and drink the wine that does not go well with certain medicines and blame the medication for their "side-effects."

This is certainly not to say that there are no side-effects. Remember, medicines are mostly intended to kill bugs, dull pain, and get rid of stop the progression of illness. Sometimes, they "throw the baby out with the bath."

It becomes essential not to live in the illnesses. That is, many allow the illness to become the person. Being a person with arthritis, is very different than being an arthritic! The person is lost to the symptoms, thus allowing a medicated body with a slowly fading mind to exist Fortunately, many persons, are able to rise above the hurts, the pains, and limited abilities of their earthly bodies and find joy in the parts that do not hurt and continue to function well.

DECEMBER

"My getter upper has gotten up and gone, but I'm still here."
— *WELBY R.*

THE LAST MONTH OF the year has many implications for older folks. It stands for another year past, one more year gone that can never return; one more year off the end, which is surely soon to come. It has joys for some, none like they used to be. But many, many beautiful old people find joy, happiness and excitement, knowing that they are the lucky ones, they are still here. Those are the lucky ones with caring family, enough money to live minimally well, and faith that makes the season a reality of hope.

No, Virginia, There Is No Santa Claus

Christmas is here. But not with much meaning anymore. Virginia did not live in a nursing home! No children to watch as their eyes gleam with excitement, no family to gather around a Yuletide feast, ears that can no longer clearly hear the carols, and eyes that cannot read the few Christmas cards they get. Every member of staff, in every facility I have ever seen, goes over and above board to make up for these losses. And they, to a very small extent, succeed. But "makeup" is only makeup, and everyone knows it.

Stoicism and faith

My dear friend, Beverly, in Florida, has been in assisted-living for several years and will likely be there until her failing body succumbs to its demise. She is wracked with pain constantly. There are no medications other than large doses of narcotics (which are not legally available frequently enough) to offer relief. Her digestive track fluctuates between constipation and diarrhea, her pulse is either barely palpable or racing. Her head is either in staggering pain or dulled into fog by medications. Her body is wasting, yet her mind is sharp. She does not complain and brings joy to everyone who visits her! Her deep faith is evident and there is no doubt that it is her constant companion. She is a role model indeed.

He Shakes, Can't See, and Has Swollen Joints

Yancy, like many elderly folks, as a matter of fact, the majority of them, does not suffer from one ailment. Many like him are plagued by multiple diseases and ailments that must be constantly addressed. They become skilled jugglers of pain, medicine, and endless doctor's appointments. Those with tremors that make self-care and eating a real challenge, those with failing eyesight who need tremendous magnification to even read the menu, those with arthritic joints that disallow most any kind of exercise including walking, those with memory deficits that keep them confused as to who they are and where they are, and. . . . . . So many more conditions. It is sometimes difficult to see the person, rather than seeing a body with illnesses. But it so important to do so.

She Gave Herself a Name

Sharon, the patient who said, "I am a diabetic," to which her doctor rightly replied, "No, you are person who has diabetes." Once one allows him/herself to become the illness, life is compromised, identity becomes a diagnosis, and the illness becomes an obsessive way of life. Deciding to remain a viable person, but a person with an illness, allows one to deal with it an "item" in life rather than the whole of their existence. What you call "it," is what it becomes with all the baggage that it carries. If have diabetes, you and your health care provider can manage. If you are a diabetic, it manages you and your life becomes a prison of obsessive psychosomatic concerns.

So much knowledge and so many skills

Homes for the aging are many times silos of incredible knowledge and warehouses of many skills. Former physicians, ministers, lawyers, engineers, teachers, homemakers, mechanics, physicists, pharmacists, and multitudes more; all endowed with tremendous volumes of knowledge. Now, it is arrested and slowly being lost. Many are still able to contribute, and would like to do so. There are not enough places that make use of these tremendous stores of knowledge. Steps need to be taken to capture knowledge and skills rather than to let it be lost to the aging process. America is not known for its respect and admiration of those who have spent a lifetime learning what they need to know.

Bitter or Better

Life in any place has its ups and downs. However, as one ages the downs are inevitable more serious and fraught with greater prob-abilities for failure and fewer resources for remediation. Many seem to think that it is aging, circumstances, living conditions, and many other things that make it so. Such is not the case. Life is a process, it is a cross-country run, not a 100-yard sprint. Life doesn't occur in a single critical moment; it occurs in the accumu-lation of how ones has dealt with previous critical moments. The bitterness, or happiness that is present in older folks, is simply the combination of how they have reacted and allowed circumstances and events to act upon them through many years.

In most instances, it is not so much what happens to them as it is how they deal with what happens. We cannot always be proactive, but we do not have to be negatively reactive either. The payoff of a positive response is not always instantaneous, but makes often makes for happiness later.

Many older people are bitter. The plague of bitterness is so ubiquitous that a whole book could be written about them. Their bitterness cannot be separated from their inner person any more than the warp and woof can be separated from a rug. By the same token, those who have maintained an optimistic attitude and life-/ style have woven into their personalities the kind of joy that transcends disappointments and the vicissitudes of old-age.

Spirituality has proven to be the key to making the difference between becoming bitter or better. Christian belief is undergirded by many Biblical texts assuring "*betterness*" rather than "*bitterness*" as we age. "He (God) will renew your life and sustain you in your old age," (Ruth 4:15); "And I (God) will be carrying you when you are old. Your hair will turn gray, and I will still carry you. I made you, and I will carry you to safety." (Isaiah46:4).

As much as I'd like to say, "it is never too late," that is a tough call. A lifetime of bitterness is difficult to change – but it can. On the other hand, unfortunately, many, particularly those without a faith base, see life as unfair and become bitter, blaming the God they do not believe in, and accusing family and friends of forsaking them, when in fact, many struggle to help them.

Some Find God

Melvin has been angry, so he says, since he was a child. Born the last of 9 children into ghetto poverty, with an alcoholic father, a mother on drugs, and two brothers already in prison, he has blamed that history. No one denies the influence of such a history or its impact. He has never been into drugs, has never been into crime or sent to prison. By the same token, neither did he graduate from high school or attend a trade school. He has had three broken marriages, which he claims were due to his unresolved anger. He maintained job, eventually becoming a manager in an industrial organization. Melvin is no 82 but no longer angry and is not bitter.

When asked, "what happened," he is quick to reply I found my inner strength in God and finally realized that I could be happy.

The Bitterness of Anger

This story to places in juxtaposition Melvin. Clare who was born into a fine, upscale home, with professional parents, and never a financial want. Plenty of everything, an only child, and doting parents. She is bitter, very bitter. She knows it but says, "my life was rotten." Whereas Melvin's life at 82 has become more vibrant, she is dying in anger and bitterness.

Clare has successfully turned nearly every part of her life into a reason to be bitter. "I never had a brother or sister, like everyone else," "My father worked all the time, and my mother was selfish," "other kids thought I was a snob," on, and on. Her choice was to allow the unfortunate events in her life to become her total focus, thus, allowing herself to morph into a "bitter old woman." She may have had a tough life, but lemonade from lemons she did not make, and how she indeed is rotting in her hatred and depression.

It's All Back There

Stanley is a truly likeable Geezer. It's just that the other Geezers know all of his stories by heart. He has only one – his life before aging, and that seems to have come rather young. He was obviously a bright, competent professional and held some quite responsible positions, but now seems to have only one story. It is made up of multitudes of trivia from his childhood. He has no present. He talks, lives, and constantly reminisces his past. He remembers the utmost details of his teachers from grade school, high school and even college. He can tell you the names of his friends back then. He remembers every building and its location in his hometown. He has no plans for the future, he has no plans for any day. All days are repeat concerts of yesterday's events.

Since none of his friends grew up around him, no one knows the credibility of any of his stories, and they morph and take on new variations each time they are told. Except that since he has told them so often, it seems that much of it is correct.

Geezer Stanely is in good physical health. You might say, "that's good." And maybe it is, but his body is apt to outlast his mind and there is no plan to take care of it. He will rot away in someplace in deep emotional pain until the brain is worn out, then suffer the indignity of an uncontrollable body until there is some merciful organ failure that ends it all.

Stanley has a wonderful father it seems and is still called "daddy." He rarely mentions a mother or siblings, although, he has spoken of them enough to know he had two brothers, one sister, and a mother. He was married and is now a widower living alone in his old home. The same house he grew up in and in which he moved many years ago when he married. Stanley represents the kind of case that causes concern. And, his story illustrates what is happening to many older folks who are "surviving" their current plight but are surely are headed for rough times since they have no purpose for the day, no plan for tomorrow, and will be too infirm to move into most retirement facilities. Then he will be dependent upon . . . who knows?

Hopefully, those who are like this will start while they still can make the changes necessary before those changes can no longer be made.

Words for Younger Folks

A few words are essential for readers who see homes for the elderly through younger eyes, and who don't yet have enough "elderly" concerns to explore living in one. The major and minor adjustments that must be made, on a minute-by-minute, day-by-day basis are totally foreign to most younger folks. Instead of the day being occupied by gainful employment, or "retirement-life," the time is absorbed with how to deal with minutia that has become all encompassing, obsessive management of major necessities.

Personal health care becomes a necessary obsession. Physical infirmities make every task a chore, physical functioning, even eating become drains on energy, and sleeping sometimes escapes life much of the time.

Brushing one's teeth, combing one's hair, putting on one's shoes, and for some simply picking up a spoon, is a major activity. The "major" activities of earlier life now become "minor" and the minor activities become major. Most folks interrupt their lunchtime, to meet a doctor's appointment. Many elderly persons must interrupt their day of doctor's appointments and medical management to eat lunch! Soon the days are the same, night and day become confused, the time of day is totally unimportant, and there is no future except to wait for the kind angel of death to relieve a miserable life.

Being blind to what the world of aging is like is not profitable education for the young. They see aging as something that will probably come but not soon. And, money, health, relationships, and living arrangements are certainly not a major concern to think about for things that might happen in the future. Money and health are the two most imperative concerns for most older folks. Although many have accumulated enough money to "last them," since no one knows how long that will be, for most it is a serious matter. Living long is costly, and most families do not have adequate financial management.

Many elderly people have few, and some no, visitors including their own family. Often, they don't concern themselves with the financial woes of even their closest relatives. They way, "mom doesn't know whether I am there or not." Often, they are wrong, since she may well know, but is not able to talk and let her feelings known. Health matters are left up to the doctors and health care staff, if they are lucky enough to live in a place where there is adequate staff. Most complaints and criticisms made by residents are written off by relatives, and often by staff, as just negative griping from incompetent old Geezers and Goozers,

Some, few by statistical observation, are able to "go to the end" with a sweet, even happy, attitude and life is enjoyable for themselves and others. It is hoped that readers who engage this writing will think carefully, give to their aging relatives freely, visit them often, laugh and tell stories, pray, sing, party, and make life a picnic, as much as is possible.

Ten Lessons You Can Learn from Old People

Compiled after many interviews with senior citizens

1. Living a life is more important than making a living. Settle for enough money to live well and be able to give to others. Chasing money ends up with it chasing you. Laugh much, learn always, love unconditionally.

2. Deciding to "live" or "thrive" in old age is your choice. You must start to accumulate your resources earlier in life. Hobbies, friends, financial security, and spiritual depth, to take you through life's inevitable adversities, and be with you to the end. Thriving is largely a choice. Even with tough financial and health concerns, one's mental attitude is key. Staying positive is absolutely essential for thriving.

3. Do not deny aging – aging well is better than staying young poorly. The physical and mental resources that permit vibrancy in earlier life gradually ebb away. Muscles deteriorate, little aches become great pains, friends forsake you, your financial status becomes a concern, and a warehouse of things you never thought of, and unimportant things become important. Start deciding on important things early in life and get them in proper order.

4. Find a doctor that practices good medicine, respects you and your body, and one whom you can respect, communicate with, and then follow his/her medical directives, and then take charge of your health maintenance. Seek as much natural and food-based treatment for physical ailments as possible. Don't try to be your own doctor but do partner with one to take charge of your daily health habits.

5. Make and maintain friendships. Tolerance is a two-way street; be glad to give it knowing you need to receive it. Relationship is the gold bullion of old age. Mend fences, forgive all, build new bridges, love one another. Don't hold grudges. Those you wish to hurt are never hurt by grudges as much as you are. They rot your soul from the inside out. Relationship is the answer to nearly all problems of aging. Relationship to family, friends, and God.

6. Practice being narapoid. Narapoid is a psychological word for the opposite of paranoid. Those who are paranoid believe everyone is "out to get them." Those who are narapoid believe that everyone is "out to help them." It is ultimate end of "Do unto others as you would have them do unto you" (Matthew 7:12). Becoming bitter or better is your choice. But you can't wait until you are old to make that decision.

7. Never lose hope. Although, definitely harder, for those with massively unfortunate backgrounds and tragic life-experiences, the death knell of life is to lose hope. It often takes conscious effort to maintain hope. Hope is easy to lose when life is ebbing away. Build it young and hang on to it through thick and thin. Even those in the horrible Nazi prison camps found that hope is king. Hope is the window when all will be better, it's just clouded over right now. For now we see through a glass darkly, but then face to face: now I know in part, but then shall I know as I am known" (I Cor. 13:12).

8. Empathize but never paternalize. Empathy is healing, sympathy is kindness but wears thin because it comes from the brain. Sharing another's burdens is different and comes from the soul.

9. Never stop loving. Evidence from psychology, medicine, and all human sciences show the power of love. Christianity ("So now, faith, hope, and live abide, these three, but the greatest is love" I Cor. 13:13), and all known religions agree that love is the ammunition against, hate, loneliness, despair, and the only foolproof medicine known to restore the soul.

10. Be grateful. Thank God for all you have, the blessings of life, happiness, friends, and health. Rejoice in your days of plenty and freedom. Your joy will be contagious!

Tips on How to Treat Old People

Compiled after many interviews with senior citizens

1. Show respect; they have lived longer and have more experience. Don't' patronize. They don't always have to be "right" to share wisdom. Treat them as equals. You may have more information and knowledge, but they have more years in the "school of hard knocks." Remember, one thing you cannot be taught but must learn is experience.

2. Be preferential; giving up your seat, offering them a hand when necessary, asking if you can help. Don't wait to be asked, seek opportunities to do good. Watch to see if an elder person needs a helping hand crossing a busy intersection, stepping up on a high curb, or avoiding the ice, or snow. Don't make them feel like a child when doing this, but as a respected and worthy senior!

3. Speak up. Most elderly persons are "hearing challenged." If you are with them, help them with phone calls – most can't understand well on the phone. Even those who "hear" with hearing aids, often hear the volume and sound but are unable to distinguish words. When asked to repeat something, don't increase your volume much, it's not the volume, it's the pronunciation, and lip reading they need.

4. Offer to run errands, shop for them, help with chores, find things they need done and do it for them. Most are too humble or embarrassed to ask for help; be proactive. Many no longer pay attention to little things that make life better. Clean their glasses, put their hearing aid in, offer to rub their back, polish their fingernails, give them a new toothbrush,

etc. They will be so appreciative that you noticed. Often un-noticed "little" things make life more comfortable.

5. Do not take money unless it is a contracted service. The re-lationship is what's being given, not the completion of a task. They, and often you, do not need the money; they, and you, need the good deed. Many older folks can't afford it, and those who can need to know that you care. Your day for returns of the favors will come soon enough.

6. For those in assisted-living and memory care: visit them! Isolation and loneliness are deadly. Read to them, play games (even if they don't understand it), sing to (with) them, play music, walk with them, look at family pictures, pray with them, tell them stories from earlier days and ask them to do the same. Be creative. Offer a foot massage! It is as good for you as for them.

7. Inquire, from staff, if there are needs that you can help meet and how you can help them make life as good as possible for your loved-one. Often elders in care do not know what they have "run out of" (toothpaste, toothpicks, nailfile, body pow-der, etc.), or what things might make life more thriving than striving. A bit of candy, some fruit, flowers, a living plant, if they are still reading, a large-print small book, and other things that if you are observant you will see.

8. Smile! Life is grim for many old folks. They have lost most things in life to smile about. Show an interest in their life, get them to talk, tell them about your life. Dig out the old pictures, it'll bring back memories, and memories are food for the soul in old age. You will both learn and laugh. Lighten up their day, and maybe yours too.

9. Listen closely. Through their partial dementia they often still maintain some gold nuggets of wisdom that just might save the day for you sometime.

10. Give thanks that regardless of your age that God has given you the breath you have, the brain you still use, and a life that brings more happiness than sorrow.

DENOUEMENT

—Joanna Sue Causley

GEEZERS AND GOOZERS IS a book of funny stories about men and women in their senior years. We will hopefully live long enough to become a Geezer or Goozer. The stories in this book I have heard throughout my life, as the authority (my father), would share and relive them with me in the voices to portray the characters. Other stories would make me think of my life and what aging would be like for me.

I am grateful to have been raised in a family where my father and mother taught that life is what I make of it, and what we have made or done with life will live long after we are gone. So, if it is tears, laughter, or stories to pass on to generations to come, may we choose to live it to the fullest realizing that each day as a gift. May we grow with grace, love, and a passion to share our experiences, called life, with others that will also grow old after we are long gone. I hope you find a bit of you in these stories, which my dad the author, has shared and put to paper. May you reflect on your life and see the stories developing that will touch others.

ABOUT THE AUTHOR

RICHARD H. COX HAS earned doctor's degrees in theology (DMin), psychology (PhD), and medicine (MD) and has been awarded three honorary degrees (DSc, DHL, PsyD).

He has served as Lecturer, Professor, Dean, and President of institutions of higher learning, including Northwestern University Medical School, Georgetown University Pelligrino Center for Clinical BioEthics, Duke University Medical School, Forest Institute of Professional Psychology, Rush University Medical College, and Harris-Manchester College of Oxford University (UK), and has published numerous books, chapters of books, professional journal articles; many original arrangements of instrumental music; as well as original paintings. He and his (deceased) psychologist wife were consultants to many retirement communities for over twenty-five years. He continues his activities now in his ninety-seventh year and lives in a retirement village in North Carolina.

Photo by Sal Lorito